VENKATEŚA SUPRABHĀTAM

Celebrating
30 Years of Publishing
in India

VENKATEŚA SUPRABHĀTAM

The Story of a Beloved Indian Prayer

VENKATESH PARTHASARATHY

HarperCollins *Publishers* India

First published in 2020

This edition published in India by HarperCollins *Publishers* 2023
4th Floor, Tower A, Building No. 10, Phase II, DLF Cyber City,
Gurugram, Haryana – 122002
www.harpercollins.co.in

2 4 6 8 10 9 7 5 3 1

P-ISBN: 978-93-5629-405-9
E-ISBN: 978-93-5629-406-6

Typeset by SÜRYA, New Delhi

Printed and bound at
Thomson Press (India) Ltd

CONTENTS

PROLOGUE

O Rama, son of fortunate Kaushalya, the eastern twilight (dawn) is breaking. Arise, O tiger among men, the morning rituals need to be performed.

With these stirring lines, Prativadi Bhayankara Anna kicked off the most famous devotional prayer extant in India. Its ubiquity in modern-day India is largely due to M.S. Subbulakshmi's (MS) unforgettable rendition that has now made it part of the morning routine in many south Indian homes. Nowadays, I often hear it in traffic jams in Bengaluru, amidst the crescendo of angrily-blaring horns, but in the past I have also heard it in less dreary places. Most startlingly, I once heard it being played on a truck with a Tamil Nadu registration plate, early in the morning at Lunkaransar in Rajasthan on the way from Bikaner to Sri Ganganagar. Getting out of a heated car on a bitterly cold morning in the middle of the desert to hear a scratchy tape-recorded song pleading with Rama to wake up makes for an other-worldly experience.

The Venkateśa Suprabhātam—an appeal for the lord to arise and save the world—is the first of the four recitations which are sung together in the morning in the temple to Lord Venkateswara in Tirumala. Regardless of whether you hear the Suprabhātam on a tape at some remote dhaba in the middle of the desert or whether you hear the massed chorus at the daily recitation during the Suprabhata Seva at Tirumala, the prayer strikes a powerful chord. Its enduring appeal lies in its evocative beauty, and in its repeated emphasis that routines of a daily life are as much a path to the Godhead and liberation, as asceticism or rituals or philosophical exegeses.

Like many others who grew up hearing this prayer, in my case in distant Delhi, my familiarity was limited to hearing the early morning taped recital. A few years ago, my father was turning eighty and I thought some piece of nostalgia about our growing up years would make for a great gift. My dad was a great one for early morning radio broadcasts, cricket commentaries during season, and Suprabhātam every day. Hence, I started exploring this prayer to see if I could gift him a translation. The quest seemed to take a life of its own. It turned out to be a difficult journey. One of the great living authorities on the subject told me, 'The Venkateśa Suprabhātam follows a ritual which is conducted in private and hence there is nothing to recount. It is a topic about which no authority will reveal inner meanings, and it is a tradition with a chronology for which no direct evidences exist.' Having said this, she still did her best to help.

The more I read, the more curious I became and the divergent paths of enquiry kept multiplying. I travelled to places, met experts and scholars, and read whatever primary or secondary sources I could find. There were many times when I wished to abandon the whole thing;

but each time I wanted to give up, a solution would emerge by itself and I would find it within myself to stumble forward. 'Sudden encounters with helpful strangers' could well be the alternate title of this work.

The title of this book itself was a happy accident. I told a close friend about this book when we had met for coffee in a café in south Bangalore. He had not heard of the Suprabhātam, though his mother is a south Indian. He walked around the café asking random strangers if they had. Not only did nearly all of them listen to it every day, but most said that it was their favourite prayer. One even sang it out to the surprise of the other coffee-drinkers. We decided there and then that it was a beloved prayer indeed.

My father's birthday came and went, but my journey within and with this poem meandered on. From being a piece of nostalgia for my father, it became a story that I had to tell my son. I hope he reads it and enjoys it as much as I have enjoyed writing it.

INTRODUCTION

Traditionally, a suprabhātam is supposed to have four sections. This book too has been organised into four sub-divisions. The first section traces the evolution of the worship of Lord Vishnu and sets the context for the composition of the prayer. The second section includes the life of the composer Prativadi Bhayankara Anna himself, and attempts to estimate the date of composition and the early history of its recitations. The third section covers the period from the sixteenth century to Independence. The fourth section traces the recitational history of the prayer since 1947. Woven through the story of the prayer are stories of the region, the system of worship, the teachers, the composers, and those who recited it.

This work is for the lay reader. Anything new that I may have stumbled upon is accidental and needs further validation. While I have tried my best to keep the spirit behind the work intact, the narrative faces the challenge of 'translation'—in several instances, literal meanings were not adequate and it was difficult to articulate relevant concepts in English. Since this is an 'external' biography of the prayer, metaphysical and philosophical digressions are outside the scope of this book—that is for the religious teachers to expound. There are few direct evidences relating to the recitation of the prayer prior to the twentieth century and hence much of the story has been inferred.

Exegesis for each verse has been offered in keeping with the 'external' nature of this work. This is based on my reading of various secondary sources. I could not find any older traditional commentary on the prayer and have relied on two recent commentaries that are in the public domain—one is a recent one in Telugu by Professor Raghavacharya and the second includes English notes of Professor Venkatacharya's translation published by the Adyar Library.

The limited goal of this work is to evoke curiosity and enjoyment about this part of our heritage.

My school-level study of Sanskrit ended in Class VIII in school. But there remained a nagging sense of a path abandoned. This lack led me to many sporadic starts in various classical languages, till I finally enrolled in Samskrita Bharati's two-year correspondence course in Sanskrit. I completed the course and was motivated to study more.

Then I enrolled for the exams conducted by the Samskrita Bhasha Pracharini Sabha, Chitoor in Andhra Pradesh—the once legendary Chitoor Board. The Chitoor Board was constituted in 1948 by a group of Sanskrit teachers and well-wishers close to the town whose name the board now bears. It seems that the founding group, in a moment of collective prescience, concluded that the standards of teaching in general, and of Sanskrit in particular, will decline sharply in modern India. They then set to define (and it seems cast in stone) a scheme of study upto the equivalent of a post graduate level which they believed would ensure continued rigour. The syllabus has not changed since then, nor has the cost of material or the course fees. Ten rupees for a textbook may have been a lot of money in 1948, but by the early twenty-first century such a fee structure is sure recipe for extinction.

The board is housed in an old building in a narrow back lane in Chitoor, Andhra Pradesh. There was a government grant at some point, but that seems to be in abeyance now. Every exam seems to be the last one the board will conduct. It is kept alive as a tribute to those who are no more, by a group of teachers whose average age is now in the mid-sixties. Of late, the board seems to have got some impetus thanks to the efforts of enthusiastic admirers but it is still a long way from recovering its old glory. Ironically, in the midst of the general resurgence in interest in the language in many parts of the country, one of the best Sanskrit courses in modern times survives largely on love and thin air. I am currently a student of this tenuous scheme of study.

This situation may be true of most classical languages in India. Sanskrit is lucky that, of late, there are many who have taken up the cudgels on its behalf, but I wonder how many folks are still left in India who can read, write, or teach one of the more obscure languages—Avestan, for example. Even within Sanskrit, knowledge of different scripts is vanishing rapidly. Almost the entire corpus of Sanskrit manuscripts in peninsular India is not in the Devanagari script. Grantha, which was widely used in south India for Sanskrit till a century ago, still has enough scholars who can read the script fluently but their numbers decrease by the day.

We don't even know the status of the lesser known scripts—many may already be extinct. In a decade or two, when the older scholars and the last of the dedicated epigraphists pass away, a massive proportion of the manuscript corpus available in India will become incomprehensible to Indians. The consequence of not studying our own heritage is that we will have to rely on the interpretations of others.

If one works diligently, the Chitoor Board curriculum is so thorough that by the time one reaches the equivalent of the Class XII (which is where I am) one can approach many original texts and their commentaries without breaking a sweat. You may struggle with a Bana Bhatta or a Dandi, but Bhartrihari and Kalidasa are accessible, and the Itihasas and the Puranas more so (though it is best to keep a copy of the Apte dictionary, the definitive Sanskrit-English dictionary, and a magnifying glass close by).

For most of its history, the Venkateśa Suprabhātam poem was a quiet semi-private recitation by a few in the sanctum at Tirumala. Its popularity in the twentieth century has ensured that it eclipses nearly all other devotional prayers—many with arguably greater devotional fervour or literary merit. MS's rendition—the obvious cause of such popularity—alone cannot explain its continuing appeal. It needed a deeper dive into the prayer's story; and that has made this journey personally satisfying.

|| SECTION ONE ||

Ideas for invoking the Almighty abound in human pre-history, and in the Indian system, such concepts eventually developed into the Vedas. The *Rig Veda,* one of the world's earliest examples of literature of any type, consists largely of prayers in praise of various deities of nature like Agni (fire), Indra (god of rain and thunder), Varuna (god of the seas), Savitr (the sun), Vishnu (the protector of the world), Rudra (the ruler of storms, pestilences and calamities, including death), Maruts (the winds), and Ushas (the dawn). The Gayatri Mantra itself is held by some to be the first in the long line of morning invocations.

As the millenia passed, these invocations metamorphosed into songs of praise to popular gods and goddesses like Vishnu, Shiva, Devi, and others. These songs are called 'stotra' which derives from the stem 'to praise'. Other derivations of this stem like 'stavaH, nutiH, stutiH' and 'stomaH' also exist as synonyms in use to mean the same as the above. Those prayers which were specifically to be recited early in the morning are called suprabhātam.

A recent commentary of the Venkateśa Suprabhātam in Telugu by the scholar K.V. Raghavacharya tells us, 'Suprabhātams occupy a special place. The Lord is in a yogic sleep. The devotee assumes the role of a loving mother to give a gentle wake-up call to the Lord by first describing the beautiful dawn that there is and the eager and hopeful world of devotees waiting for His attention and performance of His daily divine duties. Though it may sound out of place to even think of God as sleeping and having to be reminded of His duties, it must be taken in the right sense of the devotee's closeness to his chosen Lord. In fact, one should look at the Suprabhātam as a 'prayer' by the devotee to dispel the darkness of his own mind as the sun rises. Thus, his repeating of the sentence, 'tava suprabhātam', meaning 'A good morning to you, My Lord!' is in truth a plea that his morning would come too! Further, the Lord too eagerly awaits his devotee to come to him and say those words for He loves to be cherished and worshipped by his devotees, as much as they would love to be with Him!!'[1]

Raghavacharya further explains the parts of a suprabhātam as '1. Descriptions of the beauty of nature at the time of dawn 2. Reminding the Lord of his daily duties after rising 3. Praying to the Lord to take care of his bhaktas while extolling his six divine qualities 4. Surrendering to the Lord declaring that there is no saviour other than him.'[2]

This book does not follow the above theme but tries to capture the spirit in the context of the times.

The first verse of the Venkateśa Suprabhātam has been borrowed by the poet from Valmiki's Ramayana and is itself considered by many to also be the first suprabhātam. This single verse contains four elements of a suprabhātam—it describes nature by speaking of daybreak, it invokes and awakens the Divinity, it begs him to do his/her duty to the world, and it has the essence of surrender running through it.

While through the millenia that followed there were many other morning invocations, including the one that the saint Tondar Adi Podi Azhvaar composed for Lord Ranganatha at Srirangam, the Venkateśa Suprabhātam made this genre one of the most popular in Sanskrit liturgy. It became a preferred method of invocation and its popularity can be gauged by the sheer number of imitations it spawned through the centuries after its composition.

Such praise-songs were not confined to the Vedic or Puranic deities alone. A morning invocation—suprabhātam—to the Buddha has been known for at least a century now.[3] A description at the end of the prayer states that it was composed by the King Harshavardhana himself, not surprising given his eclectic approach to spiritual matters as he grew older. Harsha's Suprabhatastotra seems to have been widely circulated in the past and copies have been found as far afield as Nepal and Tibet.

Poets are composing prayers in this genre even today. The deities are varied but the broad framework that the composer of the Venkateśa Suprabhātam—the saint Prativadi Bhayankara Anna—established six centuries ago, endures.

१

kausalyāsuprajā rāma
pūrvā saṃdhyā pravartate |
uttiṣṭha naraśārdūla
kartavyaṃ daivamāhnikam ||

O Rama, son of fortunate Kaushalya, the eastern twilight (dawn) is breaking. Arise, O tiger among men, the morning rituals need to be performed.

The word 'Ram' here is used in the sense of address. 'Naraśārdūla' can be construed as 'tiger among men'.

'Daivamāhnikaṃ' means spiritual routines done during the day which are enjoined as a part of the daily routine. The word 'saṃdhyā' means twilight and since Indian tradition distinguishes between two types of twilight, it is specified here that it is the eastern (pūrva) twilight—the one which is seen before sunrise.

This verse itself has been borrowed by the poet from Valmiki Ramayana's Balakanda. In chapter 23 of the Balakanda, the sage Vishwamitra, in whose charge Rama and Laxmana were, awakens the two, who were sleeping on a bed of leaves, with this exhortation. Aahnikam comes from the word aahnam which means the day. Essentially, Rama and Lakshmana were asked to start their daily rituals.

What were the daily rituals that they were asked to perform? What did the two divine boys do when they were awakened and how did they behave differently from modern day children is a natural question.[4]

The Ramayana supplies us with details. The two woke up, bathed and then recited various mantras and prayers. They then went with Vishwamitra to the spot where the Sarayu river meets the holy Ganga. There they saw a hermitage and asked Vishwamitra to tell them more about the place. He said that the love god Kama was once burnt to death by Lord Shiva. He became formless (ananaga) and his ashes fell there. Hence this place was called Anga. The two decided to stay the night after meditating at that holy spot.

At a larger level, Vishnu's (Rama is an avatar of Vishnu) sleep is a significant aspect of his godhead. He sleeps on the serpent Adishesha at the end of every cycle of creation and destruction. Most conceptions of the god depict him asleep on the primal ocean. This is also called Yoga Nidra, a very deep meditative state.

After a period of some activity, Lord Vishnu relaxes in the company of the goddess and while doing so, allows a welcome pause to all activity in the universe. Annually, he takes his rest during the monsoon season—four months from the eleventh day of Ashada. During these four months, he stops functioning. Many occupations enjoy a period of vacation as nature regenerates.

However, his rest is normally abortive. From time to time, the god is beseeched from this happy state to ameliorate the lot of humanity.

❖

Vishnu is still widely worshipped with the name with which he is referred to in the *Rig Veda*. The name 'Vishnu' itself means the all-pervasive one—nothing, either sentient or non-sentient, can exist without him.[5] Apart from the *Rig Veda*, there are references to Vishnu in the Brahmanas, the Aranyakas, and of course, the two epics, Ramayana and Mahabharata. Many of the Puranas are dedicated to him.

The *Rig Veda* highlights Vishnu's primary nature as a liberal and a caring God who was always protective towards all creation. By encompassing the universe in three strides (in the Vamana avatar), he is symbolically the benevolent guardian who is able to grant prosperity and is called upon to remove obstacles in everyone's life. Since the order in the universe is maintained through his effort, he is also referred to as the 'cowherd' or the protector of the universe.[6]

Vishnu started being identified as Purusa and Narayana as time passed. The famous Purusa Sukta of the *Rig Veda* describes how the primordial being, Purusa, was divided and hence became the creator of all beings. Purusa himself is conceived as an impersonal creator who encompasses the entire creation and even exceeds it by the span of ten fingers. What is extraordinary about this prayer is the conception of one all-encompassing, all-powerful force which stands over and above all other divine and mortal manifestations. Added to this is the realisation that this force has to be sought within as all creation emanates from this force. With this prayer in the *Rig Veda,* the ancients articulated their concept of a single omniscient, omnipotent God.[7] The Narayana Sukta extends the Purusa Sukta with Narayana being specifically addressed as the omnipresent, omnipotent force. The prayer ends with an exhortation to all to join Narayana and meditate upon Vasudeva, and requests Vishnu to oversee the entire inner journey.

Vishnu in his form as Vasudeva and his partnership with Arjuna, were popular enough for Panini to frame rules of grammar using them.[8]

By 300 BCE, even the Indo-Greeks numbered themselves among the worshippers of Vishnu, and the most emphatic declaration of faith among these is by Heliodorus in 113 BCE. An envoy of the Indo-Greek King Antialcidas to the court of the Sunga King Kasiputa Baghabhadra, he became a worshipper of Vishnu and announced this event in an inscription carved on the Garuda pillar at Besanagar (near Vidisha in Madhya Pradesh).[9]

२

uttiṣṭhottiṣṭha govinda
uttiṣṭha garuḍadhvaja |
uttiṣṭha kamalākānta
trailokyaṃ maṅgalaṃ kuru ||

Arise Govinda, arise O one on whose flag Garuda dwells, arise, O Laxmi's beloved, and purify the three worlds.

In this verse, the god is addressed as Govinda and that may be interpreted in different ways. It can mean one who is praised by the gods whom he helped.[10] It can literally be one who looks after herds of cows.However, the word 'gō' has many meanings. It of course means kine or cattle. But it can also mean one who looks after the world as gō also means the earth. Gō also means speech, and since the Vedas are said to be the purest speech, Govinda could be someone who is sought through immersion in the Vedas. All of these are equally applicable to Vishnu. The Apte dictionary listing of the word gō and its derivatives runs through two pages.

Sanskrit allows wide latitude and flexibility if the rules of grammar are adhered to. Hence, poets in earlier times were able to convey multiple meanings through their compositions. God is also addressed as the one whose banner displays Garuda or one who has Garuda on his banner—Garuda is the preferred mode of transport for Lord Vishnu.[11] The god is being asked to awake to purify trailokyaṃ—the three worlds.

In the first verse, the Rama avatara of Vishnu was invoked. This was borrowed from the Valmiki Ramayana. The second verse is an invocation to the Krishna avatara.

❖

With worship of Vishnu gaining prominence, veneration of his wife Lakshmi, or Sri, too acquired importance. While goddesses have been revered in all cultures and societies, the Sri Sukta which is appended to the fifth Mandala of the *Rig Veda,* crystallises the concept of the Goddess Lakshmi as the wife of Vishnu and as the embodiment of nature in fifteen verses.

The Sri Sukta starts by invoking her as the one with the colour of gold, adorned by rays of the sun and the moon and being endowed with signs of prosperity like gold, etc. Invoking her makes the devotee prosperous. She is awakened by the call of elephants. Trees and plants, like the bilva and others grow due to her grace. She is referred to as kind and as the cause of fertility. She is known through her fragrance (like a flower). She stands on lotus flowers and is held up by elephants. Worshipping her brings wealth and fame.[12]

In the Vedic era, the concept of nature as a benign procreative feminine force was well recognised. Moreover, this force was seen as being intertwined with the main protective agent, Lord Vishnu.

The theme of Lakshmi as the goddess of prosperity and wealth seems to have been firmly established by the third century BCE. The Gaja Lakshmi image of the goddess, flanked by two elephants, is seen in coins that were issued in Kausambi, Ayodhya and Ujjain in that era. Even the Indo-Greeks were not immune to the allure of the goddess and it seems that she was the city goddess of the ancient Bactrian city, Pushkalavati.[13] Apparently, by then, the goddess's reputation as the harbinger of good fortune had spread far beyond—even to Rome. In 1938, a very rare ivory figurine, dated from the second quarter of the first century CE, was discovered in the ruins of the Roman city of Pompeii and was identified as Goddess Lakshmi.[14] Parallelly, in many parts of India, the rise of the cult of the Varaha avatara led to the rise of the of worship of Lakshmi as Bhu-devi or the Earth goddess. Apart from the extensive rice-growing areas in India, where her worship became widespread, the goddess, as Dewi Sri, is seen in Southeast Asia as the key divinity in aiding fertility. By the time the Mahabharata was compiled, her position as Vishnu's partner had been firmly established.

The next two verses are therefore a supplication to Lakshmi to keep a benign eye on the devotee before he or she addresses god.

३

mātassamastajagatāṃ madhukaiṭabhāreḥ
vakṣovihāriṇi manoharadivyamūrte |
śrīsvāmini śritajanapriyadānaśīle
śrīveṅkaṭeśadayite tava suprabhātam ||

> ***O mother of the entire world, O one who is sported on the chest of Madhu and Kaitabha's enemy, O ruler of the one with a divine and pleasant face. O giver of gifts to those who seek refuge (in you), O wife of Venkatesh, awake and protect us.***

In this, the goddess is referred to as the mother of the world. Goddess Lakshmi is then addressed as one who is sported on the chest of 'Madhu and Kaitabha's enemy' and one with a divine and pleasing countenance. She is the goddess of wealth and is invoked as the mistress of prosperity, wealth, and well-being. Those who seek protection are 'śritajanaḥ'—'śrit' means approached for protection or succour. In the previous verse, God is referred to as Lakshmi's husband and now the balance is being restored by referring to the goddess as Lord Venkateswara's wife.

The two demons, Madhu and Kaitabha, mentioned in the verse, have a fascinating story and there is more than one version of the tale.

One version is recounted by the sage Vaismapayana in the Shanti Parva of the Mahabharata. When Mahavishnu was sleeping in the ocean of milk, a lotus bloomed from his navel and from the lotus, Brahma was born. Brahma began the work of creating the Vedas. On the same lotus, there were two drops of water—one sweet as honey and the other hard. These two drops became the demons Madhu (who characterised tamasic qualities) and the demon Kaitabha (whose nature was rajasic).

To digress briefly, 'gunas' are attributes that are present in varying degrees in each being—all are present but one or the other predominates. There are three gunas—sattva, rajas, and tamas. Sattva guna is explained as a state of purity that results from enlightenment and a lack of morbidity, and in turn generates happiness and continued attachment to enlightenment. Rajas guna springs from passion and desire and leads to an attachment to action and craving for sensual pleasure. Finally, the tamas guna arises from incorrect knowledge and leads to negligence, indolence, and sleep—in other words, actions that detract from doing the right thing. Each of these attributes is thus both a cause and an effect of enlightenment, craving, and ignorance, respectively.[15]

Coming back to Madhu and Kaitabha; they stole the Vedas, took them to the nether-world, and brought great distress to Brahma, since the Vedas are supposed to be his eyes. Brahma appealed to Vishnu, who in this telling assumed the form of Hayagriva (the horse-headed one) in order to combat Madhu-Kaitabha. The horse-headed god then proceeded to recite the Vedas so melodiously that the two got distracted and the Vedas were restored to Brahma. They then got infuriated, took on Hayagriva and were killed in the ensuing battle. At an allegorical level, the story of Madhu and Kaitabha is a tale of the triumph of sattvic gunas over rajasic and tamasic gunas as Brahma became arrogant as the possessor of the Vedas. Lord Vishnu created Madhu and Kaitabha to help him get rid of his ego.

The other version of the tale is from the Devi Mahatmayam. At the dawn of time, Vishnu was in a state of trance-like sleep. From his ear, some earwax oozed out and it begat the two demons—Madhu and Kaitabha. Since they were born from a part of Vishnu, the two demons grew to become powerful beings. They meditated long and hard and pleased the Mother Goddess (thereby proving that they may not have been bad through and through—Indian stories have shades of grey!). The Devi gave them the boon that they would be unbeatable as long as they fought as one. Boons like these never lead to good and the duo embarked on a career of general mayhem. The climax came when they harassed Brahma and stole the Vedas. Brahma went from pillar to post but to no avail. He turned to Vishnu, but Vishnu was still in a state of deep trance. When Vishnu awoke, he fought for five thousand years against the two without success. Vishnu then flattered the duo till they agreed to confer a boon on him. He asked them to tell him how they could be killed. They honoured their commitment and despite the fatal consequences, told him.[16]

In another ending of this version, Vishnu assumed the form of Mohini, bewitched the duo, and sought a boon. The boon was the method to kill them. They said that they had to be killed in a place without water (since everything was covered with water in that time, this can be assumed to have been a reasonably safe way out for the duo). Vishnu expanded his thighs, put the duo on them, and squeezed them to death.

The Vedas were rescued. Out of the body fat (meda) of the demons, the earth was shaped and hence the name Medini for the earth.[17]

Vishnu is known as Madhusudana due to this achievement and hence is also referred to as Madhu and Kaitabha's enemy in this verse of the prayer.

❖

Driving up to Tirupati, one realises why this range of hills has had such a grasp on human imagination for such a long time. To reach Tirupati from the south-west, one has to turn off from the main highway at Chittoor and drive in the general direction of Kanipakkam. The country becomes hillier and the road undulates. Sudden vistas open up and at the same time, one suddenly descends into valleys. A slow drive, even if it means constantly dodging trucks, allows one to soak into one of the most underrated landscapes in southern India. The road passes by Pakala and enters what seems like a narrow defile between the hills. A new road is now being cut through but we can imagine the road as it was a few centuries ago. A hilly trail surrounded by forests on both sides, it would have been difficult to traverse. The hill fort of Chandragiri suddenly looms up in front. The multiple rings of walls, now in ruins, point to its important role in the past. Through the centuries, Chandragiri would have been the western gatekeeper to Tirumala, and travellers who braved the hilly roads from the south-west would have viewed its walls with relief or wariness, depending on their intent.

Crossing Chandragiri, one emerges on to the basin of the Suvarnamukhi river and the reddish cliffs of the Sheshachala range dominate the consciousness here onward. A subsidiary range rises up on the right and the traveller enters a hollow surrounded by hills on both sides. The new Tirupati bypass gets you to the foothills of Tirumala in fifteen minutes from Chandragiri.

As the Eastern Ghats extend southwards, just south of the pilgrim town of Srisailam, the Nallamala Hills rise and run through the Lankamalla range of the

Eastern Ghats and move on to the Pallakonda Hills. The Sheshachala Hills are at the southern tip of this continuously forested range. At Tirumala, the range makes a leftward U-turn and turns northeast to become the Vellikonda Hills.

The Sheshachala or the Venkatachala Hills are ancient. The base of most of the Deccan Plateau, including this range, is composed of rocks formed in the Archaean period—this was the geological eon about 3.9 to 2.5 billion years ago when life may have first emerged on Earth. When rock formation started again, after a billion years, sandstone formed and then, on top of the sandstone, a bed of shale formed.[18] The various strata of rock formations are clearly differentiated and make for a geological curiosity. This is called the Eparchaean Unconformity and is a unique enough phenomenon for it to be accorded a place in the list of geo-heritage sites in India.[19]

Perched on the escarpment of the Sheshachala Hills and overlooking the plains of Tamil Nadu to the south, the location of Tirumala cannot be more dramatic. The traditional account is that the entire hill range comprising Nallamalla, Pallikonda, Seshachala Hills, etc., is the body of the divine serpent Adishesha on whom Vishnu rests and that Tirumala is located on the crest of the hood, Ahobilam—another centre famous for its Vishnu Temple is on the back and Srisailam is at the tail of the serpent. Many of the devout, in earlier times, refused to step on the hill range as they did not want to place their foot on the divine serpent. The ecological benefit of such a belief, in preserving the biodiversity of this range, is incalculable.

४

tava suprabhātamaravindalocane bhavatu
prasannamukhacandramaṇḍale |
vidhiśaṅkarendravanitābhirarcite
vṛṣaśailanāthadayite dayānidhe ||

Awake O lotus-eyed one, O one with a beautiful face like the halo of the moon, O one who is worshipped by the wives of Brahma, Shiva and Indra, O treasure house of kindness, O wife of the lord of the Vrishaba Hill.

The goddess is addressed as the lotus-eyed one—'aravindalocane'—which is also an epithet for Vishnu. Lotus or 'aravind' means one whose form replicates a wheel with spokes.The blue lotus is actually a type of a water lily (nymphaea nouchali) that has thirteen to fourteen petals.

The next word is a thirteen-syllable compound which denotes the wives of Brahma, Shiva, and Indra into one-word, i.e., 'vidhiśankarendrāḥ'. As may be seen later, one of the names of Tirupati is the Vrishaba Hill and Lakshmi is also addressed as the wife of the Lord of the Vrishaba Hill.

The fourth verse of the poem dedicated to Lakshmi also arouses curiosity due to the metre used in its composition. Except for the first two verses which are in the eight-syllable anustup (अनुष्टुप) metre, the entire poem is in the fourteen-syllable vasantatilaka (वसन्ततिलका) metre, except for the fourth verse which is in the rare thirteen-syllable manjubhashini (मञ्जुभाषिणि) metre.

A brief digression on poetic metres in Sanskrit may be required here. Prosody is the study of metres and structures of verses, and Sanskrit prosody or chandas is one of the most important aspects of the language. It is a Vedanga—one of the six allied disciplines in the study of the Vedas. The earliest extant work on Sanskrit prosody is the Chandah-Sutra of Pingalacharya. This is a set of very terse aphorisms which set the rules for poetics and is now incomprehensible to most Sanskrit students without a commentary. The standard work that is used nowadays on the topic (and relatively easier compared to earlier works) is *Vrittaratnakaram* by Kedar Bhatta.

Coming back to poetic metres, Sanskrit composition is, in the main, either prose (gadya) or poetry (padya). A padya or a stanza is made up of four pa'ada or quarters. Each pa'ada or quarter is made up of a specified number of syllables (akshara) or syllabic instants (matraa).

A syllable is the arrangement of sound which results in speech. A syllable is built around a vowel and may or may not have an accompanying consonant. A vowel may be classed as short, long, or longer depending on the time taken in the expiration of breath while enunciating that sound.

A consonant is a syllable only when it is accompanied by a vowel. In Sanskrit prosody syllables are classified as 'big' or 'small' (guru or laghu) depending on the vowel types that are attached to that syllable and the consonants that follow. The most basic rule is that laghu syllables have short vowels and guru syllables have long vowels, and there are some other rules as well. The guru or the big syllables are depicted as '_' and the laghu or the small syllables are depicted as a U or an inverted U. I personally prefer to characterise guru as 1 and laghu as 0. These long and short syllables are further arranged in combination of threes. These combinations are called gana (गण) and there are eight of them.

In this particular verse (the fourth) of the Venkateśa Suprabhātam, there are four quarters of thirteen syllables each. A metre made of this combination is called manjubhashini. All other verses, except the first two which are in the anustup metre (four quarters of eight syllables each), are in a metre which has fourteen syllables in each quarter and is called 'vasantatilaka'. This is very curious.

Why is there a thirteen-syllable metre in the middle of a poem full of fourteen-syllable metres? Exceptional poets like Prativadi Bhayankara Anna, who composed this work, will not permit such anomalies unintentionally as the whole point of structured metres is to create cadence and harmony when the work is recited.

I thought that this verse could be a marker of some sort, or some other cryptographic device, and I spent a lot of time looking for such devices in the poem.

The futility of using methods of critical analysis on a work of devotion became apparent after a few months of such digressions. The saint composed the prayer spontaneously in a state of rapture. His sole objective would have been to pay obeisance to his personal god. The grammatical or metrical rules are a guideline but compositions that are done in a state of grace are not to be subject to these. Lifelong training in modern methods of analysis and critical enquiry are a handicap in such a situation. A journey like this becomes fruitful if the traveller were to confine himself/herself to observing and narrating, rather than to analysing and explaining. It seems to require a sense of wonder rather than a framework for analysis.

A few months ago, a possible answer emerged while listening to an older recital. I had not noticed till then that the first three verses are always recited twice. Though it cannot be said with certainty, perhaps the metric change in the fourth verse is to remind the reciters that from that verse onward, they should recite each verse only once.

❖

The main idol of Lord Venkateswara at Tirumala is self-manifested and the tradition is that the idol has been resident at this place since the dawn of time.

The traditional account of why Lord Vishnu came to reside at Venkata Hill itself resonates with his quality of compassion. Sage Bhrigu once visited Brahma, Shiva, and Vishnu to test them. While the former two ignored him, he went to see Vishnu in Vaikunta. Bhrigu found him in his usual trance-like state (could be sleep or could be a deep level of meditation—sources differ). Departing from the standard protocol of waking Lord Vishnu by singing his praises, the sage kicked him on his chest. Vishnu's solicitous response was to enquire if the sage's foot was hurt. The sage went away convinced about Vishnu's primacy. However, Goddess Lakshmi was angry at this insult. Since she lives on Vishnu's chest, it was an insult on top of an injury, so she left Vaikunta and came down to earth. She chose modern day Kolhapur as her residence. Vishnu too came to earth looking for her and reached Kolhapur. When he was worshipping her idol, he was informed by a disembodied voice to proceed twenty-two yojanas[20] south of Krisnaveni river to a river called Suvarnamukhi; there he would find his earthly abode.[21] According to Puranic stories, he stays in Tirumala for the benefit of mankind in the troubled Kali age and is called Venkateswara, or the Lord of the Venkata Hills.

There are enough evidences to indicate that the early humans considered the foothills of Tirumala a comfortable place for their settlements.[22] In the words of one authority, the Suvarnamukhi valley with 'an altitude of 150 metres above mean sea level, with an ecology, as of today, of dry deciduous woodlands, woodland savannahs, shrub savannahs and water bodies, was a most congenial prehistoric habitat in the Eastern Ghats'.[23] The tributaries of the Suvarnamukhi seem to have been particular favourites—there would have been abundant game, a profusion of wild fruits and berries, and relative safety.

Did these early men go up the hill to where the temple stands today? We do not know. While it would have been more convenient to live in the valley next to the streams and the lakes, it is probable that they may have visited the hilltops. The walkway through Alipiri, which we use currently, could have been the first easy path. It is hence not inconceivable that this 'high place', which is the source of the lifegiving streams in the valley below, would have been imbued with spiritual significance very early in human history.

The origins of the current system of worship of Vishnu lie in the efforts of a group of teachers whom we know collectively as the Azhvaars. These saints first enunciated the concept of complete surrender to the grace of god as a path to liberation. Much later, this became known as the Bhakti movement.

The Azhvaars used Tamil to sing the praise of their chosen deity and they were among the earliest devotional poets who used a vernacular language in praise of God. While many of the verses were framed in terms of the beloved waiting for her lover, their style is muted in comparison to the religious literature of the medieval period.[24] The themes were simple and related to routines of daily life. The songs they composed are unsurpassed in devotional fervour and evocative imagery.

These songs are collectively called the Naalaayira Divya Prabhandam or the Four Thousand, and were collected by the teacher Nathamuni towards the end of the first millennium. These verses encapsulate concepts which are found in the Upanishads, Brahmanas, and other scriptures. The songs are sung daily in many parts of south India and the corpus is considered as important as the Vedas.

Details of the lives of the Azhvaars themselves are a source of much discussion and the important hagiography about their lives is the Divya Suri Charitam written by Garudavahana Pandita in the eleventh century CE.

Traditionally, they are of divine origin, with different Azhvaars being incarnations of different aspects of Vishnu. Modern writers place them between the second and eighth centuries CE.[25] There were twelve teachers and according to tradition, the first three—Poygai Azhvaar, Pey Azhvaar, and Buttat Azhvaar—were born on consecutive days of the same month and year. After years of wandering in search of realisation, the three accidentally came together for shelter one rainy night in a small room in a hermitage. They were so cramped that there was barely place to stand, but each suddenly felt that presence of one 'other' who had apparently forced himself in without them knowing. To their subsequent surprise, they found that it was Lord Vishnu himself who had squeezed in and all of them spontaneously composed the songs called Tiruvandadi.[26] Another, Nammazhvaar, meditated under a tamarind tree from childhood for sixteen years till another Azhvaar (Madhurakavi) who became his disciple woke him from his trance. There are many more stories like this.

There is no doubt that the Azhvaars must have inspired a dramatic increase in the worship of Vishnu. From a prince—Kulashekara Azhvaar—from modern-day Kerala on the one hand to Tirrupana Azhvaar on the other, the Azhvaars represented the entire spectrum of society. They included saintly gardeners like Tondar Adi Podi, as well as warriors like Tirumangai Azhvaar. Such a wide representation must have also led to the adoption of Vishnu as the preferred god by many across south India as the saints were teachers with whom all could relate, and also because they taught in a language known to all.

The early history of the temple itself is lost in the mists of time and the sanctity of the hill was being celebrated in verse in early CE. From times immemorial, Venkata Hill was known as the northern boundary of Tamil speakers and was also famous for the festivals that were celebrated there.[27]

The ancient Tamils knew Vishnu as Tirumal and he was associated with God Mayon. The name Mayon itself comes from the Tamil word for dark colour and applies to both Lord Vishnu and bees.[28] His feet were specially venerated and were worshipped as a means to end the cycle of births. His chest was the seat of Lakshmi.[29] He is worshipped either in a recumbent position, seated, or as a standing image. At Venkata Hill, he is described as a blue cloud with lightning for his attire, and rainbows for his ornaments.[30]

A certain Tondaman is mentioned in the Puranic stories as the one who actually built the temple on being given detailed directions by Lord Vishnu himself. He is the subject of many stories throughout the *Venkatachala Mahatmayam*—the compendium of all Puranic sources about Tirumala. Tondaman himself would have belonged to a very ancient dynasty and his antecedents are the subject of a detailed study in one of the standard histories of Tirumala.[31] The idol is also described as one on whom the sun and moon shine, indicating that the temple could have been more in the nature of a pavilion in the days of yore.[32]

The Azhvaar saints were voluble in their praise for Lord Venkateswara and ten of them have dedicated close to two hundred verses of the four thousand to singing about Tirumala. Poygai Azhvaar describes the Lord as standing in Venkatam, and the wild elephants that infest the plantations on the hill.[33] Bootat Azhvaar continues in the same lyrical vein about the natural beauty of Tirumala, and he talks about bamboo thickets and forests in the midst of which Lord Venkateswara stood. We hear from him that even monkeys offer fresh flowers to Lord Venkateswara and elephants offer bamboo shoots dipped in honey.[34]

Pey Azhvaar strikes some of the most evocative notes. He describes Venkata Hill as the residence of the Varaḥa avatara (the boar), the bamboo groves, rutting elephants running amok, tigers prowling, and the peaks that touch the moon. He says that the rivulets flowing down the hill look like pearl necklaces. The Azhvaar even speaks about gypsies planting crops on furrows made by the tusks of the wild boars.[35] The themes of elephants, rivers looking like pearls, the temple in the midst of bamboo thickets, wild animals, tribals, gods, and asuras uniting to worship Lord Vishnu at Venkatam are continued by Tirumalisai Azhvaar and Tirumangai Azhvaar.[36] Others who mention Tirumala include Nammazhvaar, Kulashekar Azhvaar, and Andal.

ও

atryādisaptarṣayassamupāsya
sandhyāmākāśasindhukamalāni manoharāṇi |
ādāya pādayugamarcayituṃ prapannāḥ
śeṣādriśekharavibho tava suprabhātam ||

The Seven Sages led by Atri have worshipped the dawn having collected lotus-like stars from the Milky Way and are eager to surrender to the shelter of your feet. O Lord of the Sesha Mountain, wake up and protect us.

'Prapannāḥ' can be understood as those who submit themselves or surrender themselves for protection. 'Prapatti' or self-surrender is the central theme of this spiritual system, though it is very difficult to adequately understand or describe it. Its importance can also be gauged by the fact that the composer Prativadi Bhayankara Anna has introduced this concept fairly early in the narrative and has made the seven sages (the mighty beings of Indian tradition) the first in the queue of those who are submitting to Lord Venkateswara for protection.

In the prayer, the seven sages offer their prayers to Lord Venkateswara before any of the gods. The Puranic tradition is that in different ages or Yugas there are different sets of supremely realised and evolved souls who are able to act as teachers and guides to the manifest world. Their primary role seems to be to disseminate wisdom and the path to liberation to all. It is the duty of the seven sages to re-establish the correct path at the onset of every new age.

The seven sages in the current age are Vashishtha, Kaashyapa, Atri, Jamadagni, Gautama, Vishwamitra, and Bharadvaaja, and Prativadi Bhayankara Anna would have had them in mind in the above verse.[37]

The stories of these enlightened beings abound in many texts and sources. Fortunately for us, the stories of the Puranic personalities have been compiled into an encylopaedia, and this easy-to-read compendium, called the *Puranic Encyclopeadia* (PE) has been used to know more about the seven sages.[38]

Anna begins the verse with Atri, then moves on to the other sages and the same sequence is followed to describe them.

Of the many stories about Atri, a few stand out. Atri and his wife Anusuya are distinct as the trinity of Brahma, Vishnu, and Shiva are said to have been born to the duo in their various incarnations—Vishnu as Dattaatreya, Shiva as Durvasa, and Brahma as the moon. The sage manifested himself as both the sun and the moon in one of the wars between gods and demons. He is also credited with composing the fifth mandala of the *Rig Veda*.[39]

There are many Bharadvajas in the Indian tradition and the PE has listed as many as seven separate references. It does not say which one of these is one of the Saptarishis. In ritualistic salutations, he is referred to as the descendant of Angiras and Brihaspati. But he is also said to be the son of Atri. His stories are largely from the Ramayana but there are references to him in the Mahabharata as well. He is associated with the sixth mandala of the *Rig Veda*.[40]

Gautama is best known as the husband of the long-suffering Ahalya. His name means the remover of darkness. She was seduced by Indra after he changed his shape to that of her husband. Though she was an unwitting victim, Gautama cursed her to turn to stone and she was subsequently released from this curse by Lord Rama. Their relationship seems to have been fraught anyway, as on an earlier occasion, Gautama ordered their son Cirakari to kill his mother. While Cirakari was pondering over the rights and wrongs of such a deed, Gautama got over his anger and rushed back in remorse to find that all was well. Most of the stories about him are from the Mahabharata.[41]

Jamadagni is famous as the father of Parasurama. The PE describes him as a 'hermit of majestic power'. Jamadagni and his wife Renuka seem to have been a united couple despite their better-known travails (he had her put to death by Parasurama). On his death at the hands of Kartaviryarjuna, Renuka struck her chest twenty-one times and this resulted in Parasurama's vow that he would cleanse the earth of the ruling class as many times. His stories are present in both the Ramayana and the Mahabharata. As a descendant of Bhrigu, he is also known as Bhargava.[42]

There are varying accounts about Kashyapa/ Kaashyapa in Indian mythology and the identity of which one is one of the Saptarishis is difficult to determine. The Vishnu Purana reference cited earlier gives one version of the name, while the PE gives another version of the name of the Kashyapa who was a Saptarishi. In the PE version of this sage's life, he is the son of Sutapas and Prsni. His knowledge of snake poison leads him to travails which are related later. Due to a curse, he and his wife Aditi are born as Vasudeva and Devaki.[43]

Vashishtha is a dominant figure in the myths. Such was his workload that one life was not enough and he had to be born thrice. His story is also the story of his wife Arundhati and their devotion to one another is much celebrated in the Indian tradition. Many stories about this sage are about his rivalry with another Saptarishi, Vishwamitra, and this was the subject of a TV serial in the past.[44]

Vishwamitra is the most formidable among the seven sages and the teacher of Sri Rama avatara. His story is, in many ways, the story of his rivalry with Vasishtha. He started by wanting to become a great sage after Vashishtha repeatedly denied him possession of his wish-fulfilling cow, which Vishwamitra, in his earlier form as a king, wanted to appropriate. Through terrific penance, Vishwamitra transformed into a mighty ascetic. He then tried to get the king Trisanku into heaven even though both Indra and Vashishtha opposed Trisanku's entry. When his efforts seemed futile, he created a sort of 'mezzanine heaven' to house Trisanku, and to this day, the phrase 'Trisanku's heaven' means an in-between unsure state. He then spent a lot of time oppressing King Harishchandra, only because Vashishtha said that the latter was a virtuous king; this too was the subject of a TV serial in the '80s. Over a period of time, after realising that such an intense desire for liberation itself was the biggest obstacle in his path, the sage let go. Due to this detachment, he finally attained the same state of beatitude as Vashishtha.[45]

One is struck by how human-like these evolved beings were. They too were subject to normal frailties like anger and jealousy. While quick to anger, they were equally quick to forgive and make amends. Many of their lives seem pictures of marital bliss. Stories about these evolved beings are a rebuttal to theories that self-denial or narrow-mindedness is necessary for liberation.

Stories of the seven sages or Saptarishis or seven wise and capable men who found their home in the sky are pervasive in many civilisations. In some cultures, men saw the same constellation in terms of a wagon and in others as a hunt which was conducted by seven brave men.

Vedic literature refers to a set of stars called the Bears which appeared high in the sky at night and that the Seven Sages were also known as the Bears in ancient times.[46] Ancient descriptions talk of the Seven Sages as the separated husbands of the Krittikas or the Pleiades. Only Vashistha's wife Arundhati is not separated from her husband and her constant presence alongside him is a testimony to her fidelity. This may also be the genesis of the tradition of a newly-married couple looking for the star Arundhati immediately after the wedding ceremony in parts of India. By attaining the skies in the form of a constellation of stars, the Seven Sages became the bridge between humanity and the heavens.

In India, this constellation was seen in the north in the ancient times. Even as recently as 500 CE, the *Brihat Samhita* repeats that the north direction—called Kauveri after Kuvera, its guardian—was made beautiful by the seven sages who shone like a string of pearls and were guided by Dhruva, the pole star.[47]

This constellation itself is said to be fixed by or guided by Dhruva or the pole star. Dhruva, in many accounts, is the third step of Vishnu. Thus, the imagery created by poet Prativadi Bhayankara Anna in this verse of the seven sages reaching Vishnu's step at the break of dawn has its origin in the earliest conception of the seven sages by ancient Indians.

❖

Venkata Hill was part of the traditional Tondaimandalam sub-division of the Tamils. As this was the northern boundary of Tamil speakers, it was frequently contested between dynasties in the Tamil country and powers from the north. Moreover, being heavily wooded and full of wildlife, the temple on the hill would have been relatively less accessible compared to other temples. Hence, common folks would have made up a majority of the pilgrims to this temple in these periods. The temple built by Tondaman may not have survived beyond the first half of the first millennium CE.

As the Pallavas re-established their rule from the sixth century CE onward, temple building and endowments to temples again gained prominence in this part of the country.[48] The Bana dynasty ruled over southern Andhra Pradesh as feudatories of the Pallavas. An inscription found at Tirumala records the birth of a prince of this dynasty, named Vijayaditya, circa 790 CE. Further, for the convenience of pilgrims who may not have been able to trek uphill, a smaller temple was built in Tiruchanur at the foothills of Venkatachala in 826 CE by Ko-Vijaya Dantivikrama. Records of contributions towards rituals in the temple are also recorded on inscriptions. Hence, by the later part of the ninth century CE, the new temple at Tirumala must have been complete enough for it to be replicated elsewhere for the benefit of devotees who could not make what would have been an arduous trek in those days, and by 935 CE had an endowment for a lamp to be burnt in perpetuity.[49]

In 966 CE, the silver replica of the main idol of Lord Venkateswara, Manavallaperumal or Bhoga Srinivasa, was installed at Tirumala by Samavai, the wife of one of the Chola feudatories. This image was endowed with jewellery and was also offered twenty-four acres of land.[50] She appointed different officials to manage the endowments so that there would be no strife between the spiritual and temporal aspects of worship. On the date itself, there are two points of view—966 CE is the date proposed by T.K.T. Viraraghavacharya, whose work is considered the final word on the history of the temple. There are others, like S.K. Ramachandra Rao, who think Samavai's donation was earlier and place her circa 600 CE.[51] Either way, by the latter part of the first millenium, the main idol was so popular that there was a need for a smaller idol for day-to-day rituals.

The linguistic innovation of composing songs in Tamil was pivotal in the development of Vaishnavism and added to its charm. By ending Sanskrit's primacy in invocation and by using themes which resonated with all regardless of birth and upbringing, the appeal of the deity dramatically increased. Thus, the use of vernacular languages in invocation and caste agnosticism were key triggers in the spread of the worship of Vishnu.

The concept of complete surrender or Prapatti that the Azhvaars propagated meant that the path to salvation was available to every human being irrespective of caste or gender.[52]

The stage was thus set by the Azhvaars for the development of Vaishnavism in peninsular India. Their work was carried forward and given its final form—in which it is practised today—by the three great Acharyas. These were Nathamuni (circa 824-924 CE), Yamunacharya (circa 918-1038 CE) and Sri Ramanujacharya (1017-1137 CE).[53]

६

pañcānanābjabhavaṣaṇmukhavāsavādyāḥ
traivikramādicaritaṃ vibudhāḥ stuvanti |
bhāṣāpatiḥ paṭhati vāsaraśuddhimārāt
śeṣādriśekharavibho tava suprabhātam ||

The gods including the five-faced one (Shiva), the one born in the sea (Brahma), the one with six

> ***faces (Kartikeya) and the lord of the Vasus (Indra) praise your deeds in your form as Trivikrama. In a corner, Brihaspati, the preceptor reads the almanac. O Lord of the Sesha Hill, good morning to you.***

The Trivikrama form of Vishnu can be seen at the Ulaga-alantha Perumal temple in Kanchipuram. He is represented as a gigantic monolithic stone idol which is a very ancient representation of Vishnu. The Trivikrama legend is closely associated to that of the Vamana (dwarf) avatara. The demon king Bali asked the Vamana avatara for anything he wished. Vishnu as Vamana asked that he be allowed to take three steps. Considering such a boon innocuous, the demon king readily agreed. Vamana then expanded to an incomprehensible size and in the first two steps covered the world and heaven. Since there was no place left for his third step, the demon king Bali offered his head for the same. The *Rig Veda* refers to this episode and Vishnu is continually referred to as the one with the three strides.

Various forms of worship in India are influenced by the Agamas. The word 'agama' itself denotes traditional knowledge handed down by a teacher to a student. Agamas are compositions that give practical expression to concepts that are embodied in the Vedas and are a call to action. They detail steps and processes through which knowledge may be converted into practice. The other important aspect of the Agamas is that they were conceived as a means of worship for those who did not have access to the Vedas.[54] Hence, in a sense, the development of Agamas was a very early form of the democratisation of religious practices.

The Vaishnava, Saiva, and Shakta Agamas are considered the most important in modern times and, as the names indicate, these specific schools emphasise the primacy of Vishnu, Siva, and Shakti respectively.* The two principal Agamas which concern the worship of Vishnu are the Vaikhanasa and Pancharatra systems. The Vaikhanasa system is considered older and more rooted in Vedic tradition.

The word 'Vaikhanasa' means belonging to or follower of the sage Vikhanas, an ancient devotee of Vishnu, whose name implies that he 'dug within himself to meditate to God'.[55] Vaikhanasa Agama was taught by this sage to nine disciples, but only the works of Marichi, Bhrigu, Atri, and Kashyapa are now known. The tradition is rooted in Vedic practices and this ancient system of worship is practised in temples across south India.The most famous temple where this scheme is used nowadays is that of Lord Venkateswara at Tirumala.

The other school used in the worship of Vishnu is the Pancharatra system and its origins too lie in antiquity. It springs from the *Yajur Veda* and incorporates some Vedic tenets. It was a well-developed system of worship and the texts associated with it are estimated to be more than two hundred and ten.[56] The Pancharatra system which originated in north India seems to have firmly established itself in southern India by the beginning of the Common Era and went on to provide much of the basis for the formation of the Vaishnava system as we know it today. This system is used in some famous temples in Srirangam, Kumbakonam, and Kanchipuram.

---

*There are Agamas in the Buddhist and Jaina traditions as well.

The Pancharatra Agama also helped in clarifying the types of incarnation or avataras that god chose to manifest himself in and through this, a form could be given to God and his attributes. The final contribution of Pancharatra to the development and spread of the worship of Vishnu was the prescription that if properly initiated, all people, regardless of birth or gender, are qualified to offer worship. To quote an authority, '... it reveals a liberal and progressive outlook in throwing open its portals to all, irrespective of caste or sex, thus bringing within its fold even those who are excluded by tradition from the study of the Vedas'.[57]

❖

Even though the worship of Vishnu had its root in hoary antiquity and while the Azhvaars wove it into the everyday lives of people, it was still one of many creeds jostling for space a millennium ago. In that period, the peninsula was a melange of competing systems. Many types of Saivas (Pasupata, Kapalis etc.), Shaktas, Buddhists, Jainas, Charavakas, and other systems which we may not even know about anymore tried to present mankind with competing paths to liberation. The flavour of this intellectually vital period with its non-stop disputation and partisan but unfettered speech is best captured in the play *Mattavilasaprahasanam* by the Pallava king, Mahendravarman.

Nathamuni, born as Ranganathamuni, first started the task of giving Vaishnavism its modern form by collating the songs of the Azhvaars. It is said that his ancestors came from the north in the early part of the first millennium. Once, after returning from a long pilgrimage, he heard a few people singing ten prayers from the Four Thousand. He was so overcome with devotional fervour that he immediately set out to find them all. The traditional belief is that he received the Four Thousand from Nammazhvaar himself after meditating under the latter's favourite tamarind tree. The modern view is that by the ninth century CE, the Azhvaars were highly venerated and their prayers were well known to the public and what Nathamuni achieved was a singularly monumental act of compilation.[58] Whether he received the Four Thousand through divine revelation or whether he went searching from pillar to post to collect them, without Nathamuni's extraordinary exertions, the system as we know it would not exist today. For this act of compilation alone, he needs to be remembered far more than he is in modern times. He then organised them into four sections of a thousand each and set them to music.[59]

Further, he organised the system of rituals in such a fashion that the Four Thousand started being recited at every Vishnu temple in Tamil Nadu.

He was also adept at yoga, and the work *Yoga Rahasya* is attributed to him. He started the ritual of 'Araiyar Seva' where parts of the Four Thousand are performed as a stylised dance in some temples.

The story of Nathamuni's death too affirms his piety. Apparently, he mistook members of the then Chola king's hunting party for Rama and Lakshmana. He followed them on foot to the Chola capital of Gangaikonda Cholapuram and died of extreme fatigue.[60]

Nathamuni started the process of synthesis where the Sanskrit Vedas and the Tamil Four Thousand came together to define the worship of Vishnu. This was taken further by his grandson Yamunacharya and then by Ramanujacharya.

Nathamuni left detailed instructions about the education of Yamanucharya—or Alavandar as he is alternately known—for he seems to have foreseen his own death and that of his son. His most famous disciple, Pundarikaksha or Uyyakkondar, as he is now known, was given the job. Uyyakondar means 'saviour', implying that he saved the knowledge by passing it on without dilution. Uyyakkondar, in his turn, deputed his student Ramamisra to supervise Yamunacharya's training.

Ramamisra seems to have discharged his duty way beyond expectation. It also helped that Yamunacharya was a child prodigy.[61] Ramanujacharya has dominated the narrative through the centuries to such an extent that, now-a-days, Yamunacharya is largely remembered as being his immediate predecessor in the line of Vaishnava teachers. However, even a cursory study of what is known of his life shows that he deserves a far greater level of veneration.

Yamunacharya was named after the eponymous river as he was born immediately after his parents returned from a pilgrimage to north India. As a child, he stood up for his teacher Mahabhashya Bhatta and challenged Akki Alwan, the court scholar of the then Chola king, to a debate. He defeated the scholar and, as prize, won half the kingdom. He also got the title of Alavandar or 'he who came to fulfill'.[62] After a while, his old teacher, Ramamisra engineered events in such a fashion that Yamunacharya realised that his true calling lay in the spiritual realm only and he returned to his spiritual instruction.

This turn of events marks a watershed moment in the development of the system, as after his renunciation, Yamunacharya devoted the rest of his life to laying the philosophical foundations of Vaishnavism. He stated his approach to spiritual questions in his stark, take-no-prisoners style: 'This dogmatism may carry weight with (blind) believers: (but) we are non-believers in your doctrines and require logic to convince us.' In the words of an earlier historian, this is 'a most rational position which every Hindu school of thought, not excluding the author's, will always do well to bear in mind'.[63]

Of note among his well-known works is the *Gitaratha Sangraha,* which is composed in an easy lucid style, and through which Yamunacharya lays down the structure for the interpretation of the Bhagvad Gita and the rules for how it should be read. Ramanujacharya's commentary on the Gita, which defines the system, follows these rules closely.

Two of his travels are noteworthy. Once, he went to Trivandrum to visit the Padmanabhaswamy Temple and in the process missed meeting an old student of his grandfather who was apparently the only one to whom Nathamuni had entrusted the secrets of the Yoga Sutras.[64] The ex-student passed away soon after, taking the secrets with him. During another trip, he chanced upon the very young Ramanuja when visiting Kanchipuram and came away convinced that the young child would be the greatest teacher of all time. Hence, before he died, circa 1040 CE in Srirangam, Yamunacharya ensured that even if he could not do it himself, arrangements for Ramanuja's instruction were complete.[65]

Meanwhile, much before, in circa 800 CE, Shankaracharya had burst into Indian consciousness and transformed the discourse on man's relationship with the almighty. He re-established the centrality of the Vedas and used the *Prasthana Trayi** of the ten principal Upanishads, the Bhagvad Gita, and the Brahmasutra as the basis for his exposition. All subsequent teachers have stuck to his method of philosophical exegesis regardless of whom they consider the Supreme One—Vishnu or Shiva. Shankaracharya's exegesis is called Advaita Vedanta or because of its first appearance in a chronological order, simply as Vedanta.

There has been a long tradition in the country that, irrespective of personal religious inclinations, rulers have a duty to protect the practices and establishments of all spiritual practices that were prevalent in their domain. In the main, the Cholas adhered to this tradition.[66] Nathamuni and Yamunacharya worked in such an environment. There was no prosecution but there must have definitely been a sense of being in the minority. The early teachers of the Sri Vaishnava school operated and produced their best work in the margins.

౭

īṣatpraphulla-sarasīruha-nārikela
pūgadrumādi-sumanoharapālikānām |
āvāti mandamanilaḥ saha divyagandhaiḥ
śeṣādriśekharavibho tava suprabhātam ||

A gentle morning breeze wafts with the divine smells of half-opened lotus blossoms and sprouts

---

*Loosely translatable as the three foundations

from rows of coconut and betelnut palms as incense to propitiate you. Arise and protect, O Lord of Shesha Mountain.

As seen repeatedly, Prativadi Bhayankara Anna uses long, compound words and often loops two of these words together. The verbal imagery is vivid. The word 'īṣat' means less in the sense of gentleness or mildness, 'praphullam' is blossoming and therefore, the word means buds which are just opening. 'Sarasiruhaḥ' means those which grow in water. Both water lilies and lotuses which grow in water, bloom in the morning, but since lotuses are said traditionally to bloom very early, it can be assumed that the poet is referring to the sacred lotus here. 'Nārikelaḥ' is the coconut tree and 'pugadruma' is the betelnut tree which is fairly common in south India. 'Sumanoharapālikānām' is best described as pleasant avenues as sumanohara is 'gladdening of the soul', and 'pālikā' means line. 'Divyagandhaiḥ' means divine fragrances, and since the third case is used it connotes with 'saha'. The word 'mandamanilaḥ' refers to a gentle breeze. The word 'āvāti' can be taken as wafts in this context. The verb can also mean to worship so that it can be said that nature is trying to worship as the breeze wafts along.

This is evocatively brilliant poetry and a superb literary device to affirm how, at a fundamental level, spirituality is a celebration of nature. Prativadi Bhayankara Anna's message seems to be that it is up to each one of us to experience divinity in the seemingly mundane.

Other sources echo this theme. Another poem, Sri Venkateśa Seva Krama, which traces the step-by-step journey of a pilgrim from the foothills till he sees the main idol, is replete with descriptions of nature and goes even further. The pilgrim climbing up to Tirumala experiences sights and smells of trees like sal, tala (palm), tamala, sandalwood, banana, and coconut, among others.[67]

Early mornings anywhere in India are special, and south Indian mornings continue to be quiet—full of smells, and occasionally, magical. There is a profusion of barbets, coucals saunter, koels shriek, prinias throng hedges, possessive drongos compete with red-whiskered bulbuls in gardens, scaly-breasted munias still nest in bushes, and a few lucky ones can get a glimpse of the occasional golden oriole. Most people still wake up well before dawn. For a diminishing few, the half-an-hour filter coffee ritual precedes the morning walk, though many now prefer the instant variety. While there are not too many coconut trees, lotus blossoms, or betelnut palms in cities, gentle breezes do bring snatches of other scents like that of the eucalyptus, the champa, and the gulmohar. The pendulous beehives are silent. The air is crisp and impatient dogs are out towing their owners. And in most south Indian towns, in some house or shop or even in a passing vehicle, M.S. Subbulakshmi would have started reciting the Venkateśa Suprabhātam around this time.

I have tried to experience for myself the morning breezes that carry the scent of budding lotuses, coconuts, and betelnut trees, but have not had any luck so far. I did manage once—near Coimbatore—to catch the smells of coconut trees and betelnut palms. At that time, I did not quite know what fragrance was mingling with the smell of the coconuts. I was told later that it was the betelnut trees. The exact smell itself faded soon after, but after all these years, the moment remains a happy memory.

❖

Ramanujacharya (1017-1137 CE) shaped Vaishnavism as we know it today. In doing so, he altered the spiritual landscape of the country as his system and its offshoots are now among the foremost in the land. Of those whose history is known with some certainty, he is among the greatest who applied their minds to spiritual questions.

Ramanujacharya was born to Kesava Somayaji and Kantimati in 1017 CE in Sriperumbudur.[68] He was intensely precocious and by seventeen he had mastered most of the religious as well as secular literature. He then started philosophical studies under a teacher called Yadavaprakasa. The traditional accounts say that due to differences in opinion, Yadavaprakasa tried to do away with him while on a trip to Varanasi. He was miraculously saved and escorted back to Kanchipuram.[69] He was later summoned by Yamunacharya for instruction but by the time he reached, the old teacher was no more. Soon afterwards, he gave up the life of a householder and became an ascetic. He began preparing himself for his life's work and also started to organise the system of rituals and worship in Vishnu temples across the land. For the former he read and studied both the Sanskrit and the Tamil scriptures.

With his commentaries on Brahma Sutra, the Gita, etc., he provided the intellectual basis for the development of the system. With his extensive reform of temple administration and forms of worship, he paid equal attention to matters of simple faith and to the spiritual upliftment of the masses. The temples of Srirangam, Tirupati, Kanchipuram, and Melkote all benefited from his active management of their affairs. His compositions include the *Vedartha Sangraha,* the *Sri Bhashya* (a commentary on the Brahma Sutras), the *Gadya Trayam*, the *Gita Bhashya* (his commentary on the Gita), the *Vedanta Sara,* and the *Vedanta Dipa*.

Later in his life, circa 1088 CE according to one source and 1095 according to another, he went to the territory of the Hoysala king Bittideva and converted the latter to Vaishnavism. Ramanujacharya also rescued the image of the deity of Govindaraja at Chidambaram and reestablished the image in Tirupati. He seems to have spent the last few years of his life in relative peace in Srirangam.[70]

Ramanujacharya passed away in 1137. The spiritual system that he established is now called Sri Vaishnavism and its philosophical basis is called Vishishtadvaita. By expounding the scriptures to all those who wanted to know (once, famously, to a large assembly from a temple spire), by emphasising the vernacular canon, by his caste-agnosticism and recognition that merit is not hereditary, and by his insistence that liberation was available to each and every human being, he made Vaishnavism accessible to all.

Importantly, in addition to being a colossal intellect, he lived long and possessed extraordinary energy. His work ethic was such that he toiled till the eleventh decade of his life. He was broad-minded, full of empathy, and moderate in expression. From establishing codes of conduct and ritual at temples, to arguing the case for his views with anyone who wished to contest it, to welcoming dynasties into the fold, and to appointing worthy successors, nothing escaped his attention. His system of religious administration runs smoothly to this day in temples across India.

While much has been written about his religious and philosophical contributions, his role as an institution builder and a social reformer needs more study. Vaishnavism emerged as a dominant system in south India—the rest of India followed in the succeeding centuries and the core of his message reached every part of the country, albeit in different forms. His teaching—grounded in empathy, humanity, and liberalism—is as relevant today as it was a millennium ago.[71]

Tirumala itself followed the ancient Vaikhanasa system from times immemorial. Till the dawn of the second millennium, the rituals at the temple must have followed the frugal system with its simplicity and its more puritanical conception of Vishnu. Neither Yamunacharya nor later teachers, like Tirumalai Nambi, attempted any change to the system. Ramanujacharya too did not change the Vaikhanasa system prevalent in Tirumala, though he overhauled the religious practices significantly.

|| SECTION TWO ||

The Venkateśa Suprabhātam resonates vividly through the centuries as it is a celebration of nature and everyday life. Anna describes nature in evocative detail and the most mundane episodes and routines moved him to song. He celebrates birds in their cages, bees humming among flowers, milkmaids in their byres, as well as water bodies and mountains and the underlying message is that visible nature is the Invisible Divine.

In peninsular India, the Hoysala dynasty and after them, the Vijaynagar kings were great devotees of Lord Vishnu. As they concentrated political power, the period from the mid-twelfth century till the mid-seventeenth century saw an upsurge in the worship and importance of Lord Venkateswara.

unmīlya netrayugamuttamapañjarasthāḥ
pātrāvaśiṣṭakadalīphalapāyasāni |
bhuktvā salīlamatha keliśukāḥ paṭhanti
śeṣādriśekharavibho tava suprabhātam ||

> ***The pet parakeets in their cages have opened their eyes and are eating leftover fruits and milk in their cages. Their excited chirping seems like a benediction for you to wake up, O Lord of the Seshadri Hill.***

The recitation of the Suprabhātam is being done by 'salīlamathakeliśukāḥ', which means parrots that have been kept captive for pleasure or sport (pet parrots). These parrots are in the best possible cages. They are reciting this immediately after opening their eyes in the morning. Further, the hungry birds have also eaten the leftover banana and kheer from their feeding cups. Perhaps due to this, their excited chirping seems like a morning benediction to Lord Vishnu. On another note, the level of prosperity of the region must have been high if pet parrots were being fed kheer.

K.N. Dave, who combined his love for bird-watching and Sanskrit literature in the monumental *Birds in Sanskrit Literature*, devotes an entire chapter to parakeets (or paroquets as he calls them). In earlier times, keeping talking birds like parakeets and mynas as pets seems to have been popular, and the art of 'shukasarikapralapan' (conversations between a parakeet and a myna) is described in his work. The mood which Prativadi Bhayankara Anna repeatedly creates in this and in the succeeding verses is that of common everyday life in villages, and the parakeet referred to in the above verse would probably have been the common rose-ringed parakeet. Dave talks about how parakeets were trained to offer benedictions to various gods. Clearly, Prativadi

Bhayankara Anna was talking about contemporary practices in this verse.[72]

❖

Ramanujacharya's life is intimately associated with Tirumala and Lord Venkateswara. In his first visit, his uncle Tirumalai Nambi—more on him later—instructed him in the essence of the Vaishnava system through the Ramayana. He subsequently visited Tirumala more than once.

In a later visit—circa 1052 CE—his purpose was to systematise rituals and practices and also to improve the administration of the temple.

His last visit was in 1130—he was more than a century old then—when he established the Govindaraja temple to house the idol of Vishnu which was worshipped in Chidambaram as this idol had to be moved urgently.[73] This settlement grew into the modern town of of Tirupati at the foothills of the Venkatachala range.

Ramanujacharya's contributions to the temple were both spiritual and temporal. On the spiritual side, he streamlined rituals without tampering with the Vaikhanasa system, which continues to this day. The recitation of the Four Thousand began during his time and the veneration of the Azhvaars at Tirumala too started then.

The recitation of the Tamil devotional songs made worship of Lord Venkateswara accessible to the majority who were not familiar either with Sanskrit or the Vedas. Ramanujacharya ensured that his reforms endured. Various monastic orders were established by him to oversee temple affairs, and families of his disciples were settled here to spread the message. Over the next few centuries, these institutions were to play a pivotal role in the expansion of the worship of Vishnu all over peninsular India.[74]

On the temporal side, as mentioned earlier, Ramanujacharya laid the foundation of the town of Tirupati—he gave it the current name—so that those who served in the temple may have a base where they could live a normal life of householders. He reinvigorated the water bodies that were required for supplying water to the temple. He set up a code which dictated all aspects of the temple's functioning, like the methods for securing endowments, process for distribution of these endowments among recipients, appointments of a class of bachelor temple functionaries called Ekangis and segregation of duties amongst them and others, laying out of gardens to provide for flowers for worship, the custom of feeding pilgrims, and so on. No detail seems to have been too trivial for him.

With the impetus of Ramanujacharya's organisation and with the ever-increasing popularity of Lord Venkateswara, by the middle of the twelfth century CE, the temple at Tirumala started to gain even greater eminence in the spiritual consciousness of the country.

Tirumala and its associated temple had by now become significant socio-economic entities and the management of temples had evolved into an important discipline.[75] An assembly was set up at the foothills of Venkatachala to ensure that the lands endowed for temples were cared for, and to ensure that charity received for specific purposes was used as per the wishes of the donors. Tanks and irrigation facilities were scrupulously inspected and maintained. Specific officials in the Chola administration were entrusted with oversight as well as executive roles in the management of temples. There was, apparently, a local-level officer whose duties included keeping track of all rituals and procedures, endowments, management, and the transaction of all temples in the designated area. The local village assemblies too had a role in the oversight and management of temple affairs.[76]

As the Cholas declined, the entire Tondaimandalam area was in a state of political flux. In the early years of the fourteenth century, the Hoysalas tried to fill the power vacuum and, since they were staunch Vaishnavas, establishments dedicated to the worship of Vishnu benefited and the temple at Tirumala was a particular favourite.

The invasion of Malik Kafur and the subsequent forays of the Delhi Sultanate threw the entire deep south in turmoil. Muslim incursions in south India led to the foundation of the Sultanate of Madura when Jalaluddin Ahsan Khan overthrew his allegiance to Delhi and set himself up as an independent potentate. The political scenario in the lower Deccan and the Kaveri valley became very disturbed as the Hoysalas then tried to uproot the Sultanate.

The narratives of a relative of the Madura sultans are an important record of the excesses of this period. Ibn Batuta's account gives us a neutral and sometimes trenchant account of this period and in many ways underlines the maxim that atrocities in the name of religion are abhorrent to all right-thinking people.[77]

Some historians speculate that Tirumala escaped attention due to its relative inaccessibility and that the invasion route skirted the area.[78] An overlooked reason for its relative safety during this period may also lie in the stance and actions of Hoysala Vira Ballala III, whom modern historians have largely ignored. It is quite possible that the invaders were so focused on removing the threat posed by this (in the author's opinion) best of the Hoysala kings that they may not have had time for anything else. Vira Ballala's redoubt at Tiruvannamalai, another holy hill south of Tirumala, menaced the route between the newly-established Sultanate of Madura and north India. The Hoysalas had to be removed for the Sultanate to be secure, and the invaders who followed Malik Kafur expended a lot of energy in neutralising this threat. Hence, intentional or not, Vira Ballala's struggles may have well saved the Tirumala temple from adversity.[79] He paid for his exertions with his life, but by the 1350s, the sultanate too was gasping for breath.

Tirumala emerged as an oasis of calm and as a peaceful refuge in these uncertain times. The idol of Lord Ranganatha was sent for safe-keeping to the holy hill from Srirangam, and the temple afforded a haven to many from the Kaveri valley in Tamil Nadu.This further changed the character of worship at Tirumala, as many of those who came here were were steeped in the Nalayiram. While the recitation of the Nalayiram (Four Thousand) in Tirumala became popular towards the end of the twelfth century, the morning invocation to Lord Ranganatha, the Tirupalli Ezhuchchi of Tondar Adi Podi Azhvaar, may have started from this period. This recitation would later be the indirect cause of the composition of the Suprabhātam.[80]

९

tantrīprakarṣamadhurasvanayā vipañcyā
gāyatyanantacaritaṃ tava nārado'pi |
bhāṣāsamagramasakṛtkaracāraramyaṃ
śeṣādriśekharavibho tava suprabhātam ||

The sage Narada too, with his taut stringed melodious lute, sings the unending songs of your greatness. These songs are sweet, unusual, and sound beautiful in all languages. Awake, O lord of the Seshadri Hill.

The word vipañcyā means 'due to (the use of) the vipañci'. Vipañci is a type of veena. Long ago, all stringed musical instruments were called veena and could be played by plucking, or with a bow, or by striking (like the santoor). Eventually, it meant a fretted instrument which had to be played by plucking. Vipanchi veena is mentioned among one of the classes of veenas.[81] Tantrī means string. It could also be played with a bow and the bowstrings had to be taut (prakarṣaḥ) and the sounds which came from the taut strings were sweet and were the best possible accompaniment to the praises sung by the sage Narada for God. These praises sound beautiful and wonderful in all languages, as the words themselves are very melodious.

For Indians of a certain generation, the figure of Narada is synonymous with the actor Jeevan intoning 'Narayana Narayana' on screen, but there is much more to the sage than the ability to make mischief.

Narada is the son of Brahma and was born more than seven times. He was born a few times to Brahma—

once as a worm, and once as a monkey. When asked by Valmiki to describe the perfect man, Narada described Sri Ramachandra, gave a short gist of his life, and then left the poet to compose the Ramayana.

In Indian lore, Narada is devoted to Lord Vishnu and the god does not tire of putting him through different experiences in order to show him the light.

In one of the more famous stories, Narada asks for a lesson in the nature of illusion, or maya. Soon after, Narada meets and marries a beautiful lady. They have many children and acquire all the other appurtenances of a happy couple. However, at some point, a great flood comes and washes away the wife and kids. In his grief, Narada turns to Vishnu who then instructs him in illusion, attachment, and the benefits of detachment. On a different occasion, Krishna turns Narada into a beautiful woman. The woman Narada then marries a great sage and has sixty sons who all die on one day.[82] The grief-stricken widow is too fatigued to do anything and is wracked by hunger. She reaches out for a mango on a tree but is upbraided by Krishna (in disguise) for eating before the funeral of her husband and children. After more travails Narada resumes his original form and the mango becomes his veena.

Narada is very proud of his prowess as a musician and as a veena player and that too causes him to be taken down now and then. In one instance, Vishnu, tired of Narada's conceit, takes him to a forest full of wailing women with their limbs cut off and their wounds bleeding. Upon enquiring, Narada is told that these are the various raginis, or deities, of different tunes who are disfigured every time Narada makes a mistake in playing the veena. Narada returns, suitably chastised. In another episode, even the extraordinary patience of Hanuman is tested by Narada's bombast. To put him in his place, Hanuman asks Narada to rest his veena on a rock. He then sings so melodiously that the rock softens and the veena sinks into the rock. When he stops singing, the rock hardens and Narada finds that his veena is stuck inside. Hanuman asks him to soften the rock with his music, which Narada is unable to. Hanuman sings again, softens the rock, and restores the veena to Narada.

Once, in Indra's assembly, Narada tries to draw everyone's attention to flaws in the nymph Urvashi's dance by making deliberate errors in his veena recital. The sage Agastaya, who is irascible at the best of times, loses it and curses her and Narada to be a bamboo. He says that the veena will no longer be an instrument only for the divine but for mortals too.[83]

There are many Naradas in the Indian tradition. In the Buddhist system, he is one of the reincarnations of the Buddha. In Jainism, he is a Gandharva king. The name may have been a title given to different people at different times who all demonstrated similar qualities. The qualities of Narada shine through the various stories about him. He is at once a revered teacher, a humble devotee, and a great musician. His mischievousness could indicate an extraordinary intellect which possesses great intuitive gifts and the ability to articulate what most want to leave unsaid. Hence, the epithet Narada could have been used through the ages to denote undying devotion, deep learning, intuitive wisdom, truthfulness, and skill in various arts.

Acquisition of such gifts is not possible without humility and toil. That is the underlying message of the stories about this sage.

❖

Ramanujacharya's disciples were all towering personalities in their own right and descriptions of their lives is beyond the scope of this work. The centuries that followed his departure saw a significant expansion in the teaching of the system, as well as a huge increase in its adherents. In the midst of this efflorescence of spirit, Vedanta Desikan and Manavala Mamunigal stand out for their contribution and their subsequent impact on the system.

Swamy Vedanta Desikan was born in 1268 in the village of Tuppul near Kanchipuram to Anantasuri and Totaramba. He was born after his parents visited Tirumala, and hence he was called Venkatanatha. His is believed to be the incarnation of the temple bell at Tirumala. By the age of twenty, he was adept in all the scriptures and was also hailed as an expert in all skills and crafts. After a while, he went to live in Tiru Vahindrapuram near modern-day Cuddalore. His mastery was not confined just to intellectual matters—he once constructed a well to demonstrate the technique to a well-digger who wanted to check if he was indeed a master of all crafts.[84] He lived simply and spent his time reading, writing, and teaching, depending on alms for his daily needs. A dramatic episode in his life that is found in traditional accounts was his rescue of the only manuscript of a commentary on Ramanujacharya's *Sri Bhashya* along with the two young children of the manuscript's author, Sudarsana Suri, amidst the carnage at Srirangam.[85]

Vedanta Desikan composed in Sanskrit and in Tamil. He wrote more than a hundred other works in Tamil, Sanskrit, Prakrit, and Manipravalam (a mixture of Sanskrit and Tamil in this case, though Manipravalam is a term used for Malayalam-Sanskrit and Telugu-Sanskrit hybrids as well). His most extraordinary act of composition, the thousand-verse *Paduka Sahasram* was done in a few hours during the night according to traditional accounts.

According to some accounts, he passed away in circa 1369 CE, though others place the date somewhere during 1371 CE. By that time, he had overseen the reinstatement of the Lord Ranganatha idol in the Srirangam temple. Reading the accounts of his life, one is struck by the realisation that Swamy Desikan spent a significant amount of his life in great difficulty and in considerable physical danger. His indomitable will, all-encompassing empathy, and an unsurpassed intellect continue to inspire ordinary folk.

The system set up by Ramanujacharya too suffered in the general mayhem caused by the incursions from the north. Kumara Kampanna, the prince of Vijayanagara who is celebrated in literature, finally administered the coup de grâce to the Sultanate of Madura and restored the Srirangam temple to its glory in 1370-71.[86] Around the same time, Manavala Mamunigal was born in Azhvar Thirunagari in 1370.

Manavala Mamunigal, or Varavaramuni, or Saumyajamatramuni, as he is sometimes known, was the last of the great teachers from Tamil Nadu who carried Ramanujacharya's humanistic and liberal message forward in its original intent. In addition to the expected qualities of the mind, he was also said to be very good-looking and soon lived up to his early promise.[87] After a while, he moved to Srirangam, where he established himself as the leading teacher of the system. His life's work has to been seen against the backdrop of the disturbances of the previous few decades. Mamunigal must have had his hands full setting the house in order. He composed commentaries on the works of Pillai Lokacharya, a poem in praise of Ramanujacharya called the *Yatiraja Vimshati* and other works including the *Upadesaratnamala* and the *Arthiprabandha*—the last as his life ebbed away. Most of his works are in Tamil or Manipravalam.

Mamunigal's life seems to have been one of steady toil—repairing temples, restoring the system of worship, writing, and teaching. He appointed eight disciples to take the message forward, one of whom, Prativadi Bhayankara Anna, is central to this story. The true impact of his work lies in the fact that the worship of Vishnu remained a dominant system in peninsular India and elsewhere. He attained liberation in circa 1443/1444 CE, after a lifespan of seven decades.

१०

bhṛṅgāvalī ca makarandarasānuviddha
jhaṅkāragītaninadaiḥ saha sevanāya |
niryātyupāntasarasīkamalodarebhyaḥ
śeṣādriśekharavibho tava suprabhātam ||

Lines of black bees intoxicated by the storm of pollen emerge in the morning from the lotus

> ***stalks growing at the edge of ponds. Their frantic buzzing, as they hurry to serve you, with the accompanying vermillion colour of the pollen seems like a song of benediction. Good Morning and please arise, O Lord of the Seshadri Mountain.***

'Makaranda' means pollen and 'rasā' means juice which could could therefore mean honey. 'Anuviddhā' means infused with or permeated with or, in this case, it would mean intoxicated by. 'Bhṛṅgāvalī' means lines of bees. 'Jhankāragītaninadaiḥ' means with the buzzing and song of the bees. According to Apte, the word 'jhaṅkāra' which is now common parlance in many Indian musical contexts, means a 'low murmuring sound, as the buzzing of bees'. Musical concepts in India draw freely from nature—a famous example is Kalidasa's description in the play *Malavikagnimitram* of the high musical note in the call of the peacocks on seeing a cloud.

The saint suggests in this verse that the bees emerge from inside lotus stalks where they had apparently spent the night. The idea of bees sleeping inside lotus stalks seemed very far-fetched in the first read but recent research has established that the lotus actually regulates its own temperature to help out its cold-blooded insect pollinators. Apparently, only two other plant species seem to share this ability to regulate their own temperature—a trait hitherto thought to be unique to warm-blooded animals.[88] Given that the lotuses are able to keep the temperature within a narrow band and the average night-time temperatures in south India vary much more, insects could have sheltered inside lotuses in the night. This trait enables an enhanced dissemination of pollen. Prativadi Bhayankara Anna's descriptions mirror nature in more ways than is superficially apparent. Though bees are not nocturnal and would prefer to be in their hives at night, poets must be allowed their licence. Niryāti means to proceed towards.

Bees are a favourite of Sanskrit writers of yore and the corpus is replete with references to them. Sushruta, the famous physician and author of the medical treatise named after him, lists eight types of honey,[89] and from them, commentators have derived the seven types of bees that were seen in classical times. The three varieties of bees that are still well known are the wild or forest bee or bhramara, the domesticated or makshika, and the flower bee or kshudraa.

In some religious literature, their humming is compared to songs in praise of Lord Vishnu. It also likens the Vedas to bees which hum the praise of Vishnu. In some religious poetry, the black bee is supposed to be a symbol of Lord Krishna himself. Bees are, of course, most associated with the god of love, Kama and the season of spring. Kama's bowstring is made up entirely of bees and they are also attached to his flag. Their humming is supposed to be a surrogate for expressions of love. The mention of intoxicated bees by Prativadi Bhayankara Anna is a well-known literary device and they were often referred to as being intoxicated with either pollen or honey or even spring—though on observation, they seem rather abstemious, hard-working creatures. In literature, the association of bees with the jasmine flower is most common but lotus and water lilies are their favourite flowers. Their love for the lotus is such that 'alipriya' or 'beloved of bees' is an epithet for the flower. Other poets besides Anna too have used the imagery of bees resting inside lotus stalks. Bana Bhatta has used this imagery in both the *Harshacharitra* and the *Kadambari*.[90] Karttunen, who has written a superb account of bees in Sanskrit literature (and is the source for much of the above information), mentions that Mirabai thought of a bee inside a flower as someone in a cold prison.[91]

❖

Saluva Mangideva who was an energetic general under Kumar Kampanna—the Vijayanagar prince who was the eventual victor against the Madurai sultans—eventually became the governor of some parts of the empire. The greatest among Mangideva's descendants, Saluva Narasimhadeva Raya is one of those figures in history whose fame is considerably lesser than his actual achievements. His personal devotion to Lord Venkateswara also sowed the seeds for Tirumala's prominence as a spiritual centre.

Saluva Narasimha's time at the helm of affairs saw a significant increase in the number of festivals and also another spurt in building new shrines in Tirumala and Tirupati. The celebration of Ugadi and Deepavali started around this time. Many other festivals were initiated during his time. The feeding of pilgrims became a very important activity and, on festive days, food was prepared for more than four thousand people.

Saluva Narasimha also commissioned the compilation of all accounts related to Lord Venkateswara from the Puranas. This work, called the *Sri Venkatachala Mahatmayam*, was first recited by Pasindi Venkataturaivar (Jiyar Ramanujayyan) in June 1491.[92]

Narasimha alone endowed the temple with more than twenty-six villages in his reign. Narasimha's universal and inclusive vision led to the the temple rituals and participation in management becoming accessible to all, regardless of caste. The inscriptions during the period record this facet of his management eloquently.[93]

As Lord Venkateswara's reputation as a wish-fulfilling god spread, many of the political figures in these strife-ridden times started endowing the temple. Not only kings but even their feudatories and chiefs bestowed gifts on the temple. The spiritual and material benefits of the worship of Lord Venkateswara attracted an ever-increasing social spectrum as more and more devotees joined the throng at Tirumala.

Tallapaka Annamacharya lived and composed during this period. Much of what we know of Annamacharya's life is drawn from the biography written by his grandson. The traditional belief is that he was a reincarnation of Lord Vishnu's sword, Nandaka. His mysticism and his personal devotion to Lord Venkateswara led him to compose more than thirty-two thousand poems, called Sankirtanas, in praise of the god. At a run rate of more than a prayer song a day, this has to be the greatest effort in devotional composition in human history. These were etched in copper plates and while they would have been popular in their days, over the centuries, they faded from popular memory. By the dawn of the twentieth century, they were effectively lost, even though the copper plates were zealously guarded by the family through the centuries.

Annamacharya's works were reintroduced approximately a hundred years ago through the efforts of the late Sri Veturi Prabhakara Sastry. His voyage of discovery itself makes for a fascinating tale. He started his work on Annamacharya's compositions in the late 1920s when he was working in the Government Oriental Manuscript Library in Madras. When the Tirumala temple came under the aegis of the Tirumala Tirupati Devasthanams, the Oriental Research Institute was established in Tirupati and Prabhakara Sastry became the Reader in Telugu. From 1940 till his death in 1949, he published many of Annamacharya's Sankirtanas.[94] After him, the great scholar Sri Rallapalli Ananthakrishna Sarma carried on the work. By themselves, Annamacharya's compositions are among the greatest corpuses of religious music composed by any one individual in the world and their role in spreading the worship of Lord Venkateswara must have been immense.

Thus, the fifteenth century marked a turning point in the history of Tirumala in many ways. In Saluva Narasimha and his feudatories, it found a devoted and munificent set of benefactors. The recitation of the Nalayiram was firmly established in Tirumala. Tallapaka Annamacharya's songs brought Vishnu into everyone's daily spiritual consciousness. Pasinidi Venkataturaivar began the recitation of stories about Lord Venkateswara found in the Puranas in the form of *Venkatachala Mahatmayam*. The descendants of Ramanujacharya's disciples had established an elaborate system for dissemination of his teachings and many of them were spiritual preceptors to the various ruling dynasties in the geography.

Early in this 'century of Tirumala', during a visit to the temple, the saint Manavala Mamunigal asked his disciple Prativadi Bhayankara Anna* to compose the Venkateśa Suprabhātam.

११

yoṣāgaṇena varadadhnivimathyamāne
ghośālayeṣu dadhimanthanatīvraghoṣāḥ |
roṣātkaliṃ vidadhate kakubhāśca kumbhāḥ
śeṣādriśekharavibho tava suprabhātam ||

In the cowsheds and byres, the wives of cowherds are speedily churning fresh milk. The vessels and churning sticks seem to fill all directions with loud clatter as though competing for your attention. Arise and protect us, O Lord of the Sheshadri.

An interesting grammatical device is employed here. In some specific types of compound words, the resultant collective noun for a group of people is a masculine even if the noun refers to a group of ladies.[95] In this verse, the collective noun for the wives of cowherds is in the masculine gender. 'Ghoṣāḥ' means villages occupied by cowherds. In this context, it probably means streets or parts of a village where the cowherds reside, as

*Hereonwards P.B. Anna or just Anna (elder brother in some south Indian languages). Some of earliest print editions of the Venkateśa Suprabhātam carried a verse stating that he had composed the prayers on the direction of his guru Manavala Mahamunigal (or Ramyajamatrmuni)—see the Introduction in Prof. Raghavacharya's Telugu commentary.

villages made up only of cowherds would have been very rare. 'Ghośālayeṣu' hence means inside houses in streets where cowherds reside. The poet plays with the word ghoṣāḥ. One means places where cowherds reside and the other means a type of loud sound. It is combined to give a sense of loud sounds emanating from the houses in the cowherd quarter of a settlement in the morning. The poet tells us the source of this loud sound is the noise of the churning stick when the churning speeds up. This speedy churning is required to get the best curd. The rest is imagery of how even the vessels vie for the god's attention and is also a good way to say that the day has begun in many houses and among different types of people.

Humankind, across cultures, derives a certain bucolic comfort from the activities of milkmaids and dairy farmers. The scene being described by P.B. Anna can be experienced even today across rural south India. Instead of pots and pans of different shapes, there are the standard cooperative society milk cans. Instead of the legendary breeds like the Punganur dwarf or the Ongole Gidda which would have thrived in the region, there is now the hybrid Jersey cow, and instead of the lady of the house, the school-going kid may be doing the milking. But the spirit of an early morning ritual, which may be mundane yet is critical for well-being, endures. Anna weaves this daily discipline beautifully into a timeless description of the rural landscape early in the morning and uses it to underline the discipline of the morning invocation.

❖

Hagiographies are scarce in India, and in English even more so. Fortunately for us, the life of Prativadi Bhayankara Anna has been documented in an English pamphlet by the late Professor V.V. Ramanujan. This pamphlet was given to the author by the saint's descendant who currently officiates at the Sitarambagh Temple in Hyderabad.[96]

Before his passing, Ramanujacharya had appointed seventy-four teachers to take his message forward. One of them was Mudumbai Nambi, who was also his brother-in-law. P.B. Anna was born in Mudumbai Nambi's family in 1362 CE. He was named Hasthigirinatha in tribute to the Lord Varadaraja of Kanchipuram.

The saint was exceptional in every way from early childhood and was soon accepted as a student by Swamy Nayana Varadacharya, the son of Swamy Vedanta Desikan.[97] As a boy, Swamy Hasthigirinatha seems to have been intellectually outstanding even by the dizzying standards of those times. He got a chance to prove himself very early. A famous scholar, Narasimha Misra, once came to Kanchipuram and challenged Nayana Varadacharya to a debate on theology and philosophy. The condition was that the loser and his students would accept the winner as their teacher. Steeped as he was in his father's detached asceticism, Nayana Varadacharya did not want to indulge in such polemics and initially ignored the challenger. Narasimha Misra misconstrued detachment for weakness and pushed for the debate.

The young Hasthigirinatha decided to take up the cudgels on behalf of his teacher. It must have been an extraordinary thing to do for a teenaged boy, combining as it did a high sense of self-abnegation and self-esteem;

self-abnegation as he chose to present himself as a shield for his teacher and self-esteem as he must have been very confident of his own prowess.

The devout draw parallels between this debate and that of Yamunacharya's debate with Akki Alvan a few centuries earlier. There seem to have been enough similarities—the relative youth of both Yamunacharya and Anna, the towering reputations of their respective adversaries, the initial deriding of both in the assembly by their older opponents (Narasimha Misra ridiculed the adolescent Anna by saying that marriage and debate are best between equals), and their eventual victory in debate.[98]

Just as Yamanucharya became known as Alavandar, or the Conquerer, after his victory, Swamy Hasthigirinatha earned the title 'Prativadi Bhayankaram', or one who is the terror of his opponents in debate, from his happy teacher. P.B. Anna may have composed his seventy-three verse praise to Swamy Vedanta Desikan—the *Saptati Ratnamalika*—after his win as the last verse mentions this title.[99]

Over time, P.B. Anna moved to Tirumala and started serving Lord Venkateswara by preparing the water required for his worship every day. This is an important step in the ritual. It was a physically gruelling task as the water bodies were often at a distance from the temples—for example, the Akash Ganga which P.B. Anna used is now a ten-minute jeep ride to the edge of reserved forest. Once the water is collected, it had to be scented with cloves, cardamom, camphor, and other such essences.

The traditional account of Anna's move from Tirumala to Srirangam is miraculous. Once, while filling the water pot at the Akash Ganga Pond at Tirumala, he met a traveller from Srirangam and the two started talking. The devotee from Srirangam narrated stories of the saint Manavala Mamunigal and his extraordinary life in Srirangam. P.B. Anna was deeply moved on hearing about Swamy Mamunigal's devotion and was so absorbed in the tale that he completely forgot to scent the holy water needed for the ritual.

As is well known, temple rituals have very precise timings, and in Tirumala, then and now, there is no flexibility on this front. An assistant (Ekangi) rushed out and grabbed the water pot from the dawdling P.B. Anna's hands and proceeded with the service. Anna realised that he had not scented the water and tried to correct it but was too late as the service had started. While he was waiting remorsefully, the officiating priest finished the service and mentioned to Anna that the scent of the water was unprecedented and almost divine. Miraculously, the water had become fragrant as it seems that the life of Manavala Mamunigal was so pure that just the recitation of his life and work was good enough to scent the water. Anna decided to be his disciple and departed for Srirangam with his family.

१२

padmeśamitraśatapatragatālivargāḥ
hartuṃ śriyaṃ kuvalayasya nijāṅgalakṣmyā |
bherīninādamiva bibhrati tīvranādaṃ
śeṣādriśekharavibho tava suprabhātam ||

The swarms of bluebottles fly out from the hundred-petalled lotuses who are the sun's friends.

> ***In their eagerness to overpower the lustre of the blue lotus in Lakshmi's hand, their humming and booming seems like kettledrums being played in the morning to awaken you.***

Here lotuses are described as friends of the sun as they bloom at dawn. They are also described as having a hundred petals. Swarms of bluebottles emanate out of lotuses in the morning—there must have been a lot of competition among insects to secure their spots inside the lotuses. The sound of their buzzing seems like the roll of kettledrums in honour of god. Further, with their blue colour, the poet says that they seek to rival the blue of the blue lotuses which are almost like an extension of the goddess's hands.

While P.B. Anna's early education must have steeped him in classical Sanskrit literature, he could not have overlooked the imagery of bees in the Prabhanndams either.

❖

After some time, Mamunigal visited Tirumala with many others, including P.B. Anna. At that time, the Tirupalli Ezhuchchi must have been sung in the temple due to the influx of the many who were serving at the Ranganatha Temple at Srirangam. On finding that there was no morning song for Lord Venkateswara, Mamunigal instructed Anna to compose one.

The composition may have been a spontaneous one in a state of grace. Apart from the twenty-nine verse Suprabhātam, P.B. Anna also composed an eleven-verse Sri Venkateśa stotram, a sixteen-verse Sri Venkateśa prapatti and a fourteen-verse Sri Venkateśa mangalasasanam thus totalling seventy verses in all.

These are recited together every day today, and together, these four prayers comprise the complete recitation.

Swamy Mamunigal then enjoined that every day, except in the month of Margazhi (approximately mid-December to mid-January), the Suprabhātam must be recited at the time of opening of the temple.

Anna became a favourite disciple of Swamy Manavala Mamunigal and was one of the Asta Diggajas (eight important teachers) assigned to take his message forward. Apart from the Venkateśa Suprabhātam and the three other accompanying prayers and the seventy-verse eulogy of Swamy Desikan, Anna composed Suprabhātams to each of the 108 other holy places of Lord Vishnu that were celebrated by the Azhvaars. Apart from these, he wrote brief commentaries to the Sri Bhashyam of Ramanujacharya, the Bhagavatha Purana, Ashtasloki of Parasara Bhatta, and the Yathiraja Vimsathi of Mavala Mamunigal. His numerous other compositions include a eulogy to Manaval Mahamunigal called the *Varavaramuni Sathakam*.

He passed away in 1455 CE.[100]

The traditional laudatory verse about Anna (known as 'Taniyan') is found among the colophons at the end of some manuscript versions of the Venkateśa Suprabhātam. To digress a little, a colophon is a very brief description of the author / content of a manuscript and / or an inscription and is very helpful in these types of quests. The laudatory verse reads as below:

vedānta deśikakaṭākṣa vivṛddhabodhaṃ
kāntopayantṛyaminaḥ karuṇaikapātraṃ
vatsānvavāyamanavadyaguṇairupetaṃ
bhaktyābhajāmiparavādibhayankarāryaṃ[101]

As a teacher who was initially taught by Vedanta Desikan's son and later by Manavala Mamunigal, Anna's worldview was non-sectarian and universal. Hence, one of the reasons for the Suprabhātam's abiding popularity could be that it is an invocation that appeals to anyone regardless of sectarian, caste, or religious affiliation. More than anything else, that is Anna's greatest legacy.

During most of Anna's own life, the rule of the Vijayanagar kings ensured stability. But the wars of the preceding decades must have been fresh in memory and would have shaped the worldviews of all. Anxiety may have been ever-present among the populace but actual physical discomfort would have been occasional and would have alternated with periods of plenitude. A prayer like the Venkateśa Suprabhātam in such turbulent times would have been an escape from the anxieties of everyday life and, at the same time, a celebration of the present.

Anna's family continued his tradition of exceptionalism and service to society though the centuries. His descendants occupied important positions at the Tirumala temple and the generations after him were so venerated as religious teachers that they are collectively the subject of a laudatory poem called the *Vādibhīkaraguruparamparāślokāḥ*.[102]

In the last hundred years, they have shone in different fields too. One of them was a freedom fighter whose name was used as a pun (Bhayankarachari) to describe the fear he caused among the British. Amidst the endless lists of Bengalis and Punjabis held captive in the Cellular Jail in Port Blair, his name—Prativadi Bhayankaram Venkatacharya—is the only entry from

Andhra Pradesh and a library near Kakinada is all that remains to commemorate his stirring feats. The most famous of them all in the last century has been the popular playback singer, P.B. Srinivas. Like his illustrious ancestor, his songs (including devotional renditions like the Mukundamala) have given joy and hope to many.[103]

१३

śrīmannabhīṣṭavaradākhilalokabandho
śrīśrīnivāsajagadekadayaikasindho |
śrīdevatāgṛhabhujāntaradivyamūrte
śrīveṅkaṭācalapate tava suprabhātam ||

O Protector, O Beloved Giver of Boons, O Friend of the Entire World, O Abode of Lakshmi, O Paramount Ocean of Kindness, O Divine presence on whose chest the Goddess of Good Fortune resides, O Lord of Venkatachala Hill, Good Morning to you.

This verse is full of mystical allusion and is an enumeration of the many qualities of Lord Venkateswara.

While the various names of Venkatachala are dealt with in a later verse, a modern commentary on the Suprabhātam relates the story of how Garuda brought Venkatachala to earth as a part of the explanation of this verse. It says that in the beginning of the epoch of the white boar, Lord Vishnu assumed that form to slay the demon Hiranyaksha and to extricate Mother Earth from the nether world where Hiranyaksha had hidden her. Lord Vishnu brought her up by lifting the earth by his canines, to place her back in the proper orbit. In the new epoch of creation, the Lord wanted to make the earth his abode so that he could care for all her inhabitants, and he bade Garuda to move his mountain which he used for sport in Vaikunta and which was named Venkata to the Earth. He had it placed on the banks of the river Swarnamukhi.[104]

This is one version of how Vishnu's abode, Venkata Hill, came to earth.

❖

The year of composition of the Venkateśa Suprabhātam itself cannot be stated with certainty, but date-range estimates can be attempted

Hagiographies about Manavala Mamunigal are extant and the *Yateendra Pravana Prabhavam* (YPP) is the widely-accepted standard work.[105] The YPP mentions Mamunigal's visits to Tirumala, though it is difficult to ascertain exactly when these took place.[106] By all accounts, Anna composed the Venkateśa Suprabhātam at the behest of Manavala Mamunigal as Swamy Mamunigal felt that instead of the Tirupalli Ezhuchchi, Lord Venkateswara should get a suprabhātam for himself. Swamy Mamunigal further instructed that the prayer be recited every day except for the month of Marghazi (roughly mid-December to mid-January) and so it has been ever since.

This prayer could therefore have only been composed when both Manvala Mamunigal and Anna were in Tirumala together. V.V. Ramanujan, in his homage to Anna, describes the journey and the sequence of temples that were visited by Manavala Mamunigal during his visit to Tirumala with Anna and his other disciples, but the period is not clear.

An old article on the development of Vaishnavism after Ramanujacharya states that Manavala Mamunigal finally settled in Srirangam around 1425 CE.[107] If we consider the story of Anna's life as narrated by Prof. Ramanujam, he would have probably become a disciple of Manavala Mamunigal before this time. From 1432 CE onwards, Manavala Mamunigal began a series of scintillating discourses in Srirangam, explaining the various commentaries of the Four Thousand. These are now recognised as one of his greatest contributions to the system. His only major travel seems to have been to the south in the period. As noted earlier, he passed away in 1443-44.[108]

Since Anna became his disciple later in life, and as Manavala Mamunigal does not seem to have travelled north of Srirangam after 1432 CE, this year could be the latest limit of the time-range within which the Venkateśa Suprabhātam could have been composed.

The first service of the morning is the Visvarupa Seva, and before the fifteenth century, it may have been a silent and private ritual. The first donation towards providing for 'prasadams' during the 'ushakala puja' or the prayers at the time of rising, seem to have been instituted only by 1434 CE.[109] Given Mamunigal's instruction, a daily recitation of the prayer must have started soon after it was composed. Endowing this service and the recitation would have been considered meritorious. Potentially, this endowment of 1434 CE further reinforces the later end of the date range mentioned above (i.e., 1432 CE).

However, the YPP gives us other clues which can help us try to estimate the earlier limit of the date-range for the composition. It says that Swamy Mamunigal appointed Koil Keetkum Emperumaanar Jeeyar—one of the officiating positions in Tirumala.[110] The probable year of composition of the Suprabhātam could coincide with the year of appointment of this Jeeyar as Manavala Munigal was instrumental in both events.

A recent history of the priestly families who supervise the rituals at the Tirumala temple has enumerated the line of succession of the Jiyars from the time Sri Ramanujacharya started that specific monastic order, as recorded in the temple inscriptions and as recorded in the Jiyar Matham—their seat at Tirumala. While the names of seers as per the inscriptional records and the names as per the Matham records do not match, it mentions that in 1420, Satakopa Ramanuja was appointed the Jiyar. The Jiyar preceding Satakopa Ramanuja Jiyar was appointed in 1385 CE and the succeeding Jiyar in 1471.[111] Thus, this Jiyar would have been the only one whose appointment fell within the active lifespan of Manavala Mamunigal. It is, therefore, possible that he is the Emperumanar Jiyar mentioned in the YPP. Given the mismatch between the incriptional records and the Matham list, the dates cannot be established with surety. It is possible that his appointment could have happened in the year that Manavala Mamunigal visited Tirumala accompanied by many, including Anna, and that year could be 1420 CE. However, till the various dates are reconciled this cannot be stated with certainty.

Putting all the above pieces of circumstantial evidence together, one can conclude—though not with certainty—that the Venkateśa Suprabhātam could have been composed between 1420 and 1432 CE.

In the year 1456, Saluva Narasimha, who was by then styled as a 'Mahamandaleswara', donated a village called Alipuram in Chandragiri for the purpose of funding a daily prasadam, or food offering, early in the morning. The summary of inscriptions calls this the 'udaykalasandhi', or the prasadam, offered at the time of arising. An inscription recording this gift was carved into the wall of the temple and gives details of the gift as well as the ingredients which were used for the offering.[112] The contents of this gift are generous, and if a personage as grand as Saluva Narasimha were to have made an endowment specifically for the time of awakening, then surely that service must have been significant. It is thus within the realms of possibility that, by 1456, the recitation of morning prayers, including the Suprabhātam, would have become an important ritual in the daily schedule of the temple and would have merited specific donations for its conduct.

१४

śrī svāmipuṣkariṇikāplavanirmalāṅgāḥ
śreyo'rthinoharaviriñcisanandanādyāḥ |
dvāre vasanti varavetrahatottamāṅgāḥ
śrīveṅkaṭācalapate tava suprabhātam ||

Shiva, Brahma, along with the four Kumaras whose limbs have been purified by bathing in the sacred tank, Pushkarini and been hallowed by the touch of your staff, stand at your door, desirous of obtaining blissful liberation.

'Haraviriñca' is a compound word for Shiva and Brahma. 'Sanandanādyāḥ' are the four Kumaras—Sanaka,

Sanatkumara, Sanadana, and Sanatana—that are born of Brahma's mind and are depicted as four children. In some sources, Sanatsujata is given as an alternate name for one of the Kumaras. They are a symbol of purity and learning and go through the universe with the sole purpose of teaching methods of salvation.

The sacred tank Swami Pushkarini is just next to the temple and a dip is customary before the devotee proceeds to the sanctorum. The devout believe that the sacred tank is the microcosm of all the holy rivers, streams, ponds, and other water bodies in the world. It is more than a sum of parts and the best description is found in the English introduction to an edition of the *Kainkaryaratnavali,* a mid-nineteenth century poem on the temple: 'The puskarini lotus pond at Tirumala comprises of various compartments with different types of wells and pools in different depths to obtain supply of water in the pond in all seasons. In the middle of the pond is the ... "pavilion"' which is made use of during Jalakrdamantapotsava, etc. To the south of this mantapa, the pond is called Svamisarovara and to the north is called Varahaka. In the Svamisarovara there are six wells sunk. These six wells are now covered with mud; but their masonary lines are still seen when the water is dried during summer for cleaning the pond. The name Varahaka for the northern half of the tank is because it lies opposite to the Varahasvami Temple. In this Varahaka pool, there is a small pool lined with masonary in granite stone. Depending upon the depth it is conceived as composing of three pools. Thus in total there are nine tirthas (sacred pieces of water) in the Puskarini. The elaborate and strenuous efforts to ensure water storage through natural springs of water on mountains stand testimony to the zeal of the bygone devotees.'[113]

Stories about the tanks and ponds in Sheshachala, their holy qualities and the benefits to be derived from bathing in them, are found in all the Purana sections collected in the *Venkatachala Mahatmayam*. The Brahmotara Purana section in the *Venkatachala Mahatmayam* provides details. The sage Durvasa is asked by King Dilipa to explain how many holy waterbodies are there in Sheshachala. The sage replies that there are sixty-six crore water bodies all over the Sheshachala range. While everything sensate and insensate in Sheshachala is imbued with divinity, 1008 of the water bodies are particularly holy. Bathing in 108 of these will give the right knowledge. Bathing in another sixty-eight will lead to devotion and detachment. However, liberation can only be attained by bathing in specific waterbodies. These are Swamipushkarini, Viyat Ganga (Akash Ganga), Papavinasha, Pandu Teertha, Kumaradharika Teertha, and Tumburu Teertha. The sage says that bathing in these will surely lead to liberation.

The ancients spent a lot of time in addressing the issue of water and finding sustainable ways to store and manage the resource. The *Venkatachala Mahatmayam* is, in some ways, a chronicle of the water bodies in the Tirumala hills. The main topics related to water bodies and their locations, benefits of bathing and/or drinking from these, myths, stories and legends, the best time to visit, and the number of water bodies. There are other small asides, like the benefits to those who protect water bodies (two verses), the Suvarnamukhi river, etc. Out of the total of more than ten thousand verses in the Mahatmayam, at least 20 per cent relate to these topics. The highest percentage of verses on water bodies is found in the Skanda Purana section, which has extensive descriptions of all holy places in India, with some sections almost entirely devoted to water bodies. The Garuda Purana and Markandeya Purana sections too have a very high percentage of verses on water bodies. The sheer number of water bodies which are mentioned in the *Mahatmayam* tell us how important the Venkatachala Hills would have been as a watershed in a region which is otherwise largely arid.

Imagine a time when the first humans stumbled through the desolate Deccan Plateau and first looked upon this verdant range of hills. It may even then have been teeming with ponds, streams, and waterfalls (crores of them, according to the *Mahatmayam*), with abundant flora and diverse wildlife. Amidst the arid desolation of its surroundings, these hills would have seemed like heaven, and that primordial memory would have, over time, transformed itself into that of Vaikunta itself in the mortal world.

❖

During the reign of Krishna Deva Raya, the Vijayanagar empire reached its zenith. Even today, devotees who visit Tirumala see the timeless evidence of his devotion for Lord Venkateswara in the form of his statue and those of his two wives in a glass showcase near the exit. He visited the temple seven times during his rule, as per records.[114] He had a particularly fraught time in the run-up to his kingship, with relatives trying to blind him, among other things. He came to the throne in 1509 and the trend of thanking Lord Venkateswara for achievements with generous donations may have well started with him. His wives too vied with one another for god's grace with gifts of equal value.

Krishna Deva Raya was particularly happy about his victories over the Gajapati kings in Orissa, and from 1514 to 1517, each visit of his to Tirumala was marked by lavish gifts, culminating in the gilding of the Ananda Nilaya Vimana. It is said that he visited the temple in 1518 to celebrate the impending birth of his son.[115] During his reign, as many as twenty-four of his feudatories too made generous contributions to the temple,[116] as did a host of religious personages, merchants, and general devotees. Doing service for the temple and instituting rituals and endowments was no longer only the prerogative of the mighty.

In contrast to Saluva Narasimha's fervent attention to almost every religious and secular detail of the temple, Krishna Deva Raya's devotion was of a deep and a personal nature—his epic Telugu poem, *Amuktamalyada*, is about the wedding of Lord Ranganatha of Srirangam with the Azhvaar saint Andal. The king himself was balanced in his spiritual outlook and his inscriptions eschew sectarian references. He helped the saint Vyasatirtha found his matha. There does not seem to have been an entourage during his visits—just his wives and few personal attendants.[117] No religious or temple functionary seems to have attained any undue influence during his rule. Krishna Deva Raya's personal munificence set the tone for the future. His last visit to Tirumala for which there is a record occurred in 1521. The departure of this enigmatic personality, both a scholar and a soldier, circa 1529, paved the way for a few centuries of general confusion.

Tallapaka Annamacharya's son Pedda Tirumalacharya (1458-1554) lived through the reigns of Krishna Deva Raya and of his brother Achyuta Deva Raya—the golden age of the Vijayanagar empire. His father had instructed him to continue the work of composing poems in praise of Lord Venkateswara and he did so for most of his life. [118] He was an ardent devotee of Lord Venkateswara and a towering scholar in his own right.[119] He continued the tradition of reciting the morning prayers as a part of his daily service to Lord Venkateswara.

The Venkateśa Suprabhātam must have influenced Pedda Tirumalacharya deeply, as sometime in his life, he composed a prayer in the dvipada metre called Sri Venkateswara Prabhatastavamu—a morning prayer to Lord Venkateswara. This Telugu equivalent of the Venkateśa Suprabhātam was rediscovered by V. Prabhakara Sastri in Madras and he had it published in 1946. Another longer version was discovered among manuscripts preserved by the family and a new print version is being planned. Additionally, there are several compositions around the theme of the Suprabhātam that can be found in copper plates and in palm leaf manuscripts.[120]

Thus, not only were the Tallapaka family reciting the Venkateśa Suprabhātam, they were also composing vernacular versions for broader transmission. Apparently, within a century of its composition by Anna, the prayer had become popular enough to inspire vernacular forays around the same theme.

१५

śrīśeṣaśailagaruḍācalaveṅkaṭādri
nārāyaṇādrivṛṣabhādrivṛṣādrimukhyām |
ākhyāṃ tvadīyavasateranisaṃ vadanti
śrīveṅkaṭācalapate tava suprabhātam ||

The Lord's abode has many names and the main among them—Srisesasaila, Garudachala, Venkatadri, Narayanadri, Vrishabhadri, and Vrishadri—are incessantly recited by your devotees. O Lord of the Venkatachala Mountain, arise and protect.

The fifteenth verse is an enumeration of the more popular names of Tirumala—the abode of Lord Venkateswara—'Srīśeṣaśaila', meaning Sesha the serpents' hill, 'garuḍācala' or Garuda's hill, 'Senkaṭādri' or Venkata's hill, 'Nārāyaṇādri' or Narayana's hill, 'Vṛṣabhādri' or Vṛṣabhā's hill, and 'Vṛṣādri' or Vṛṣā's hill are the more popular names of the range.

Known by many names during the various ages, Tirumala itself means sacred hill in Tamil and now, in the Kali Yuga, it is called Venkatadri. It is called Garudadri as Garuda carried it from Vishnu's abode, Vaikuntam, to Earth.

The *Venkatachala Mahatmayam* has all the details on how it came to be where it is and the stories behind its names.

The holy hill was called Vrishabhadri in the Krita Yuga. Once upon a time, there lived a demon by the name of Vrishabhasura, who took over the sacred hill. This demon, like other of his ilk, spent his time harassing all other ascetics but was also a tremendous devotee of Lord Vishnu. His particular form of penance was quite novel. Every day, he would go to the Tamburu Pond and after bathing there, would cut off his head and offer it to the Narasimha avatara. His head would miraculously grow back. He kept this up for five thousand years till Lord Vishnu, impressed by the devotion, manifested himself and asked Vrishabhasura what he wanted. Vrishabhasura said that he did not want mundane boons like salvation nor the world's overlordship but instead sought the gift of a battle with the lord himself. 'So be it' was the laconic response and they commenced hostilities. To everyone's surprise, Vrishabha held his own and matched the lord, move for move. Then Lord Vishnu assumed his vishwaroopa, the form where he encompasses the universe, to combat Vrishabhasura and asked if he had anything to say before he unleashed his discus Sudarshana to kill him. Vrishabhasura told the Almighty that death by Sudarshana Chakra was the surest path to salvation and therefore his strange request for battle. He asked that after his death, the sacred hill which was the lord's dwelling on earth be named after him. His wish was granted and hence, among the villains in Hindu mythology who were called Vrishabha (others being a brother of Sakuni and a demon who was killed by Krishna), he is remembered with fondness and reverence each time the name Vrishabhadri is uttered.[121]

In the Treta Yuga, the hill was called Anjanadri. The monkey king Kesari and his wife Anjana were childless. In distress, Queen Anjana went to the sage Matanga and requested him to propose a solution for her childlessness. He suggested that she go to the sacred hill where she would find a sacred pool called Akash Ganga. Bathing in that pool, he said, would help her fulfil her desire. She immediately proceeded there, bathed in Akash Ganga, and offered penance. Then, through the grace of the wind god, she conceived a son shortly thereafter. This was the great Hanuman. Since Anjana offered penance here to beget a son, this hill is also called Anjanadri. There is another Anjanadri near Hampi, the site of the mythical Kishkinda. That too is said to be the site of Hanuman's birth.[122]

Once, Vishnu was resting in Vaikuntam with his wife, after instructing Sesha, the serpent, to stand guard at the entrance. At that point, the wind god, Vayu came to seek an audience with the One Who Sleeps on the Ocean of Milk (i.e., Vishnu). When he tried to enter Vaikuntam, he was stopped by Sesha and an argument ensued between the two.

While they were arguing, Lord Vishnu himself came there. Sesha insisted on a contest with Vayu to ascertain who was stronger. The contest was that he would hold on to a beautiful, gem-adorned, holy mountain called Venkatachala and if Vayu had the strength, he would have to uproot that mountain, a son of Mount Meru. Sesha anchored himself to Venkatachala and the wind god started blowing with ever-increasing speed. His power was such that he uprooted and flung Venkatachala, along with Sesha, fifty thousand yojanas away, towards a spot which was on the banks of the river Suvarnamukhi. The suitably chastised Sesha then offered penance for a thousand years in order to propitiate Vishnu. Vishnu was suitably gratified and finally appeared before his penitent mount. Sesha said, 'O Lord! If I have satisfied you, please grant me this boon. Just as you rest on my body in Vaikuntam, please rest on this hill which too is my body on Earth.' Vishnu replied, 'Long ago, when I was contemplating a beautiful place on Earth for me to sport, the great sage Narada visited me. I asked the Best among the Ascetics who had come from Earth to suggest a likely spot. He replied that there is a certain hill known as Venkata which is equivalent to Vaikunta and is suitable for your residence. Know that what transpired is ordained and I will grant you your boon of resting myself on your earthly form as well.'[123] In the Bhavishyotara Purana section, there is another version.[124] Vayu still shows up at Vaikunta and tries to force entry, and Sesha still stops him, claiming to be the favourite of the Almighty. The difference in this version is that Lord Vishnu himself suggests the contest (to further his divine will) and asks Sesha to bind the peak of Mount Meru using the coils of his body as a rope. Thus, the hill is called Seshadri in the Dvapara Yuga.

In the age of Kali, the hill is called Venkatadri. Once upon a time, there was a learned devotee called Purandara who had a son called Madhava. Madhava grew up to be learned and an able scholar in his own right. He was married to a beautiful and worthy bride called Chandralekha. One day, Madhava overcome by desire for his wife, importuned her during the day. The lady demurred initially stating that the daytime ritual (agnihotra) was being performed and his parents were nearby but eventually agreed and asked him to meet her by a nearby pond. On the way to the pond, Madhava saw another beautiful and desirable girl called

Kuntala. Overcome by desire for Kuntala, Madhava importuned her instead. Kuntala argued long and hard that it was wrong of a person like Madhava, who was married, to suggest what he had. But Madhava would not listen and eventually forced himself on her. Kuntala angrily insisted that he leave his wife and stay with her. They lived together for twelve years, after which she died. Madhava lost his mind and wandered around like a lunatic. Then inadvertently, he joined a group of pilgrims and reached Seshachala. On just stepping on the Seshachala Hill, he vomitted violently and all his sins were vomitted out and destroyed. Hence, the hill got the name 'Ven' plus 'Kata' which means the destroyer of all sins.[125]

❖

Achyuta Deva Raya succeeded his illustrious brother Krishna Deva Raya in 1530. He had been kept confined in the Chandragiri fort for most of the latter's rule. Perhaps it was Krishna Deva Raya's way of ensuring loyalty and only after his young son died was Achyuta Deva Raya permitted to share power as part of the new succession plan. At the same time, the king's son-in-law, Aliya Ramaraja too seemed to have been given a prominent role in the administration. The last five years of Krishna Deva Raya's reign thus saw the beginning of a contest between the two, which was to have fateful consequences for the empire.

Keeping relatives in close confinement for long periods to blunt their competitive edge was apparently a common practice among kings in many places, and this confinement is used by some to explain Achyuta

Deva Raya's nature and his shortcomings.[126] Other scholars, however, contend that he was a well-meaning and gentle person who tried his best under difficult circumstances, and point to his achievements in his short reign.

In the long years of his confinement, Achyuta Deva Raya spent most of his time worshipping Lord Venkateswara. The Tirumala temple could be seen from Chandragiri and the tough climb to the temple, up Srivari Mettu which starts near Chandragiri, could have been his daily shortcut. When he unexpectedly came to the throne, his change of status from a political detainee to an emperor must have seemed like a miraculous deliverance; among those who have ruled in the peninsula, there are few who have been as fervent a devotee to Lord Venkateswara as was Achyuta Deva Raya. His devotion was such that he even insisted on conducting a ritual himself—an act which must have caused a lot of confusion among the priestly ranks. He started his military campaigns with a sequence of visits to holy places, the first of which was Tirumala. He called his son Chinna Venkatadri as he believed him to be a boon from Lord Venkateswara. In terms of munificence, he was again without equal. Achyuta Raya even set up a town, a temple, and a tank in his own name in Tirupati but, apparently, divine will was contrary to this and remnants of these locations are now hard to find—there can only be Lord Venkateswara in Tirumala and Govindaraja in Tirupati.

Apart from kings, even their ministers were great devotees of Lord Venkateswara and patrons of the temple. One of them, the Pradhani Timmarasa, created an endowment in 1535. Over a period of time, due to the travails of time and change in personal circumstances—some accounts hold him responsible for Krishna Deva Raya's son's death—he transferred his share in the temple's prasadam to Tallapaka Tirumalayyangar subject to the latter fulfilling some conditions. Sadhu Subramania Sastri, the pioneering epigraphist of the Tirumala Tirupati Devasthanams (TTD), speculates that these conditions probably related to the recitations during the early morning service (suprabhata) or those late at night (ekanta),[127] and it is likely that his conjecture may have actually been the case. If so, this would be one of the first markers of the recitation of the Venkateśa Suprabhātam by the Talapaka family. Later inscriptions recording the donations of Pedda Tirumalacharya circa 1545 CE record that the Tallapaka family further appointed others to sing the Sankirtanas in their stead, and perhaps the recitation of the Venkateśa Suprabhātam as well.[128] Subsequently, the family resumed the recitation themselves.

The reign of Krishna Deva Raya and Achyuta Deva Raya saw a period of extended peace in the peninsula. The general tone of royal devotion must have motivated people across the social spectrum, ranging from powerful feudatories to dancing girls, to create endowments for the worship of Lord Venkateswara.[129] The donations kept pace with the increase in devotees and it is estimated that during Achyuta Deva Raya's reign, donations to Tirumala increased threefold.[130]

The tradition of invoking Lord Venkateswara as a witness for commercial transactions between parties may have started around this period. There is an inscription in the Govindaraja Temple at Tirupati which describes a contract between cloth merchants and lease-holders (contractors). The penalty for non-conformance to the terms of the contract was a fine which was payable as an offering to Lord Venkateswara. Apparently, tightly worded clauses and God's grace were enough to ensure sanctity of contract between the parties—the state or the king are absent in this transaction.[131] Thus, by now, Lord Venkateswara's abilities as a wish-fulfiller were acknowledged equally by kings and commoners, regardless of religious denomination.[132]

|| SECTION THREE ||

With the death of Achyuta Deva Raya in circa 1542, the political consensus among the noble families that had been pieced together during Krishna Deva Raya's rule started wobbling and the dormant rivalry between the various factions in court came to a boil. Achyuta Dev Raya's son Venkatadri was a collateral casualty of this internecine strife. The Aravidu family of nobles eventually prevailed in the succession feud and Sadashiva Raya—a nephew of Krishna Deva Raya—was crowned as king in 1543.[133] Krishna Deva Raya's son-in-law, Aliya Ramaraya, became the real power behind the throne. Sadashiva Raya's devotion to Lord Venkateswara was great, and though his munificence was muted in comparison to his immediate predecessors, the Tirumala temple continued to inspire sustained philanthropy among the lay public. The empire reached its furthest extent—stretching from coast to coast and from Orissa to Kanyakumari.

Aliya Ramaraya is now known in history as the loser at the battle of Rakkasa Tangạdi/Talikota but many accounts also talk of the good that he did for the empire and of his contribution to its improved administration. The encounter at Talikota in 1565 ended the purple patch of the Vijayanagara empire and the life of Aliya Ramaraya.

Ramaraya's brother Tirumala, who escaped the ensuing slaughter with the greater part of the treasure and the captive king Sadashiva Raya in tow,[134] became king and ruled till circa 1572 when his son Sriranga I took over.[135] However, the disruption to the established order was such that for eighteen years from the battle of Talikota, it seems that the authorities at Tirumala were not sure whether the Vijayanagar kingdom existed or not.[136]

Rituals at the temple must have been impacted, though evidences are few and far between. The story of the Venkateśa Suprabhātam from this period onwards till the early part of the twentieth century can only be inferred.

१६

sevāparāḥ śivasureśakṛśānudharma
rakṣombunāthapavamānadhanādināthāḥ |
baddhāñjali pravilasan nijaśīrṣadeśāḥ
śrīveṅkaṭācalapate tava suprabhātam ||

Your premier servants, the Protectors of the eight cardinal points—Shiva, Lord of the Gods (Indra), Krishanu (Agni), Pavamana (Vayu), Lord of the Waters (Varuna), Protector of Dharma (Yama), the Lord of Wealth (Kubera), and Niruthi, who are themselves refulgent in their halos, wait upon you

with folded hands on top of their heads. O Lord of the Venkatachala Hill, good morning to you.

The ancients were very well versed in the eight points of the compass and believed that each cardinal point was guarded by a divinity. These divinities gave their names to the directions and are collectively called the Dikpalas or the Dikpalakas.

Shiva in his form of Ishana is the guardian of the north-eastern corner. He is one among the trinity who are the principal deities in the Hindu system as we know it today and does not need any introduction.

Agni is the guardian of the south-eastern direction and his seat is called Tejovati. He is the god of fire, and apart from being a guardian of the direction, he is one of the five elements. He is the agency through which offerings in sacrifices reach gods. Agni is next to Indra in importance in the Vedas, and the Puranas are full of stories about him. Since, in Vedic times, fire was created by rubbing two sticks together with the help of air (seems logical, as oxygen is important for fire), Agni is also said to be the son of Vayu, the wind god. Since he comes to earth from heaven in the form of lightning, he is also said to be born of the clouds.[137] Discovering fire was the most important step in the evolution of human beings and our myths capture collective memories of that important event—nature was the basis for religion from the earliest times.

Indra guards the east. He was the most prominent in the *Rig Veda*. As Vajrapani, he is foremost in early Vedic traditions as one who helped people overcome their enemies. In Puranic lore, he declined in importance to being the king of the gods and stories about him abound. He constantly runs afoul of some sage or another and gets cursed as a penalty. At various times, he becomes a bull, a calf, a fox, a goat, and a woman. More than any other deity in the Hindu pantheon, he represents human frailties and passions best.[138] In his Purandara form, as a destroyer of cities, he is depicted in some rare idols with a hammer or a mace. As the god of thunder, with lightning as his weapon, he would have been the one that ancient humans, in awe of the inexplicable forces of nature, would have feared the most. His primacy in the Vedas may be due to this primordial fear and the resultant need for propitiation.

Yama, the god of death, guards the south. He is also called Kala. When a living being's time is up, he (or his trained assistants) fetches the person and then determines their next stage. When Sri Rama's time on earth ended, Yama was sent to do his duty and this must have been his toughest assignment. Yama disguised himself as a great sage and asked to see Sri Rama alone to tell him a secret. Lakshmana was posted at the door with orders not to let anyone in while Yama was speaking to Sri Rama. As the two were conferring inside, the sage Durvasa showed up hungry after a penance of a thousand years. He demanded to see Sri Rama and to be fed and threatened to curse the entire race if he was denied (as we have seen, this sage is fast on the draw with imprecations). Lakshmana went in to inform Sri Rama, and as self-penalty for disobeying orders, drowned himself in the Sarayu. In remorse, Sri Rama too followed him into the depths, allowing Yama an easy way out.[139]

Kubera, the god of wealth, is the guardian of the northern direction. He is also the brother of Ravana who threw him out of his splendid abode in Lanka and appropriated his wealth. Kubera kept making more money and grew rich again. His capital is Alakapuri, which is also the abode of many semi-divine creatures. One of these was exiled to a hilltop in central India and became the central figure of Kalidasa's *Meghadutam*. Kubera was beset by Ravana on other occasions and he once escaped in the disguise of a chameleon. He is a particular friend of Shiva's, who protects him often. Kubera lent a lot of money to Lord Venkateswara and to this day that debt is being paid off by the donations of devotees who throng Tirumala.[140]

Varuna, the god of water, guards the west. He is depicted as carrying a rope and riding a horned shark. He was gifted the bow 'Gandiva', later gifted to Arjuna as a result of Agni's prayers. He waxes and wanes with the moon. Unlike many of the other gods who steal the possessions of various sages, Varuna had his cow stolen from him by the sage Kashyapa.[141]

Nirrita guards the south-west and is a very enigmatic deity. He is depicted carrying a sword, seated on an ass or on the shoulders of a man. He is the son of Sthanu.

Vayu, the wind god, guards the north-west. He is born of the breath of Visvapurusa, according to the *Rig Veda*. His contest with Sesha, the mount of Lord Vishnu, resulted in the Seshachala Hill reaching its current location. Both Bhima and Hanuman are his sons and he is one of the few major deities who is overshadowed by his offspring.[142]

❖

The next few decades after Talikota saw increasing confusion in peninsular India. Sriranga I generally had a tough time and was followed by Venkatapati Raya (Venkata II) from 1586 to 1614. Venkatapati moved his capital from Penugonda to Chandragiri, perhaps to be even closer to Tirumala in these times of stress—he was the viceroy of this area under the reign of his brother Sriranga.[143] His twenty-eight-year rule is now hailed as a period of peace as he arrested the decline of the empire to some extent. His policies were proactive and, despite many challenges, he even regained some territory. It seems that a gong was placed near the summit of the Tirumala Hill, and this used to be sounded to tell the kings at Chandragiri that Lord Venkateswara had received the prasadam. The kings would eat only after they heard the sound of the gong.[144] While Venkatapati Raya is acclaimed as one of the most devoted servants of Lord Venkateswara, his relative poverty led to very few new grants during these years, and most were by way of improvements of irrigation infrastructure.[145]

By the early part of the seventeenth century, the focus of worship seems to have shifted to Tirupati.[146] The death of Venkatapati Raya led to the now routine carnage among the court factions. Sriranga II became king in 1614, but was soon murdered and Ramadevaraya (Rama IV), who had escaped from the accompanying massacre by being hidden in a pile of laundry, was anointed as the titular emperor in 1616 or 1618 CE.[147] During this time, the various feudatories of Vijayanagara who had started carving up dominions for themselves emerged as independent political entities. The Matla family had its moment in the sun around this time and the greatest among them, Matla Kumara Anantaraja, performed many acts of devotion at Tirumala, including building the Gali Gopuram, which is on the footpath to the temple. Rama's death in 1632 led to another round of blood-letting, and after a decade of general confusion during the rule of Pedda Venkata Raya (Venkata III), which among other things saw the English acquire the rights to the future city of Madras, Sriranga III emerged as the last Vijayanagara king in 1642.

Meanwhile, once their treaty with Shah Jahan removed the threat to their northern borders, the southward thrust of the Deccan sultans became urgent. The European merchant companies were also becoming players on the political stage. The chieftainships of Madurai, Tanjore, Senji (Gingee), Mysore, and Ikkeri, which were to play a critical role in the affairs of the peninsula in the next century, became prominent in this period. The political environment of the time was a confused melange of ever-changing alliances and there was considerable flexibility of principle in the pursuit of fixed purposes. The Vijaynagar kings were under constant pressure. Sriranga III began his rule and spent the next couple of decades in a desperate effort to hold on as the titular head of the remnants of the Vijaynagar empire. With the loss of the fort of Udayagiri through the enticement of its commander, Sriranga III's position became terminal and Muhammed Sayid, the victor, was appointed the Mir Jumla (head of government) of Golconda by Sultan Abdullah Qutub Shah in 1643.[148] For a while, Sriranga III and Golconda forces alternately controlled the area around Tirupati.

१७

ghāṭīṣu te vihagarāja mṛgādhirāja
nāgādhirāja gajarāja hayādhirājāḥ |
svasvādhikāramahimādhikamarthayante
śrīveṅkaṭācalapate tava suprabhātam ||

In the valleys of Seshachala, all your mounts, Garuda, the Lord of Birds, Sesha, the Lord of Snakes, the Lord of the Animals, Ucchishrava, the Lord of the Horses, and the Lord of the Elephants have completed their respective roles as determined by you and are supplicating you to arise and protect the world.

This verse describes the various mounts of Lord Venkateswara.

The mounts of Lord Venkateswara are best seen at the Brahmotsavam festival, which is one of the most ancient and important festivals in Tirumala. The word 'utsava' means 'the removal of all sorrows and inauspicious things'.[149] Traditional accounts trace the origin of this festival to Brahma. Troubled by the depredations of the demons, Brahma prayed for deliverance and, in response to his prayers, Lord Venkateswara sent his discus to kill the asuras. In gratitude, Lord Brahma himself initiated the festival. The *Venkatachala Mahatmayam* has extensive details, and in the Varaha Purana section, we find mention of the divine animals that are vying with one another to bear Lord Venkateswara during the festival, which is currently celebrated over nine days. Ucchaisrava, the divine horse, the elephant Airavat, Ananta, the serpent, and Garuda, the lord of birds, take turns to bear him during the festival.[150] The first inscription recording the Brahmotsavam dates back to 966 CE and records a grant for the festival by Princess Samavai, whose munificence apparently touched every facet of the worship of Lord Venkateswara. Endowing Brahmotsavams later became a popular, if expensive form of thanksgiving to Lord Venkateswara. By the end of the fourteenth century, there were seven Brahmotsavams in a year, and a couple of centuries later the number had grown to eleven. The use of the vahanas also seems to have multiplied according to the wishes of the donors.[151]

By the time Anna composed this prayer, the generosity of the devotees meant that the procession of the vahanas as a part of the Brahmotsavam would have been almost a monthly feature in Tirumala.

Garuda, the eagle mount of Vishnu, is a popular icon in the cultures of many countries. Indian mythology has numerous stories about him—numerous enough to be included in a separate work by itself [152]—and one of the Puranas is named after him. His abiding qualities are strength, determination, and beyond it all, a sense of renouncement. Before the start of the Brahmotsava festival, Garuda invites all seen and unseen divinities and powers that live in and around Tirumala to come and attend the festival. The Garuda vahana was used on the fifth night of the festival from 1530 CE[153] and that event is considered one of the most auspicious in Tirumala.

Sesha or Adishesha or Ananta is the divine serpent who is the seat of Vishnu when he is resting on the ocean of milk. Devotees of Lord Venkateswara can thank Sesha for being the inadvertent cause of Tirumala

Hill's current location. On the evening of the first day of the Brahmotsavam, a flag-hoisting ceremony takes place, and later in the night, the deity, along with his two consorts, is taken on a ride in a vehicle called the Pedda Seshavahana. A smaller one called the Chinna Seshavahana is used on day two and this is supposed to represent Vasuki—another divine serpent.[154]

Simha refers to the lion mount of Lord Venkateswara, and is used on the third day of the Brahmotsavam festival. An inscription from 1614 CE mentions the use of a silver Simhavahana.[155]

Uchhaishrava is the mythical horse which was one of the beings who emerged when the ocean of milk was churned by gods and demons. His form was said to be so entrancing that even the gods were beguiled.[156] A golden horse was presented in 1628 CE by Matla Kumara Anantaraja—he seems to compete with Samavai in terms of his range of endowments.[157] This vahana is used on the eighth night of the festival.

Airavata is the son of Iravati and is the divine elephant. He is supposed to have been both the cause and an effect of the churning of the milk ocean in different myths. The Gajavahanam, or the elephant mount, is used at night on the sixth day of the Brahmotsavam.[158] Inscriptions from 1583 and 1628 CE speak about this.[159]

This verse also implies that in the Seshachala Hills, universal peace and amity prevails among creatures that would have otherwise been inimical towards one another. The flora and fauna of the Seshchala Hills have long been celebrated in verse. The Azhvaars were lyrical in their descriptions of the hills. Kulashekar Azhvaar wants to be a stork in the sacred pond, a fish in the pools, a bee, and finally, a wild stream in Tirumala. Tirumangai Azhvaar, in his *Periya Tirumoli,* is particularly evocative about the natural wonders of Tirumala. He talks about the tanks and ponds brimming with red fish, the trees that are bent over with dew in the mornings, the rustling groves of bamboo, and the flower groves that resound with the humming of bees. His repeated description of how the clouds rub the ground resonates with many who have experienced misty mornings in Tirumala in the decades past.[160] Elephants had disappeared from Seshachala for many decades. But as seen earlier, the Azhvaars described them eloquently when singing about Venkata Hill and it is certain that elephants roamed the Seshachala Hills from time immemorial. Hence Anna's description of elephants in the valleys of Seshachala is apt. Since 1993, it seems that a herd has taken up residence in the Chamala valley of the Seshachala Hills and the population seems to have grown subsequently. Nature has come a full circle.

❖

Aurangzeb renewed the Mughal territorial expansion towards the south and the Mir Jumla, Mohammed Said craftily used this opportunity to defect to the Mughal camp. The resultant strife between Golconda and the Mughals could have been Sriranga III's chance for a comeback, and the Europeans, from their perches on the coast, sensed an impending change in the status quo. However, the moment passed as Sriranga III was poorly served by his followers. His devotion to Lord Venkateswara remained intact till the end, and in 1665, there is an inscription which seems to be beseeching God for help—too late for him in any case. The control of the area around Tirumala passed to Reza Quli Beg, titled Neknam Khan, and he seems to have tried to calm the situation.[161] Meanwhile, the revenue administration of Golconda and other parts of Deccan had been completely taken over by Hindu accountants and many rose to the higher reaches of the Golconda administration. The Telugu-speaking brothers, Maddanna and Akkanna reached dizzying heights and some speculate that they actually ran the Sultanate. Their influence could have kept Tirumala free from unwanted interference.

Aurangzeb's foray into lower Deccan and the reprisals of the Marathas saw the whole region descend into further chaos. Through all the mayhem, Tirumala remained untouched. Nicolo Manucci speculates: 'It seems to me the reason for not doing so (i.e. attacking the temple) was his (Aurangzeb's) fear of renewed rebellions.'[162] Thus far, Lord Venkateswara's grace had protected his devotees. For the next couple of centuries too, their devotion kept his temple at Tirumala safe.

Chatrapati Shivaji swung past Tirupati in 1677[163] and Akkana recorded a visit to Tirupati in 1681, which may have been his last as soon afterwards he and his brother were assassinated. By this time, the situation in Tirumala was grim and there would have been just enough for the most rudimentary requirements. The tribute being paid out must have been taking a toll. There were very few left at the temple and even they seemed indigent—a far cry from even two centuries ago when even temple grandees were great philanthropists in their own right.[164] As may be imagined, even conducting regular services at the temple would have been a challenge. There would have been a handful of priests and other functionaries living in danger and under constant tension. Most would have had to make the trek up the hill to Tirumala every day before dawn through the wildlife-infested jungles to serve the temple and return to an unsure existence every evening. The flow of devotees would have reduced to perhaps a trickle. This period would have been the lowest point in Tirumala's history.[165]

Given disturbances and paucity of inscriptions, evidence of recitation and temple rituals from the beginning of the seventeenth century onwards, when the Vijayanagara empire was waning, are hard to come by. As visits to Tirumala became more and more difficult for the common pilgrim, it is possible that in this period, rites and rituals of the temple may have been mirrored in individual homes. Thus, while there is no direct evidence to support this, the Venkateśa Suprabhātam itself seems to have spread beyond the temple as recitation of the prayer became part of the daily routine of householders in parts of south India. Manuscript copies would have been made as an aid to recitation as the laity may not have been as thorough in memorising the prayer as the temple's servants.

Scanning the different manuscript repositories and their catalogues seems the only way in which one can know anything at all about the story of the Venkateśa Suprabhātam in this period.

Stories of early surveys and collection drives for manuscripts can fill many volumes and are outside the scope of this work. It would suffice to say that Indians of all stripes should be intensely grateful for the effort that was put in. Many surveys and collections have not yet been completely examined. For example, Colin Mackenzie's collection of records in peninsular India, undertaken towards the end of the eighteenth century, may even now throw up new sources of information. Sustained work started in the middle of the nineteenth century, and by the 1880s, Gustav Oppert drew up lists of Sanskrit manuscripts in private libraries in south India—he lists four manuscripts of the Venkateśa Suprabhātam in his survey.

१८

Sūryendubhauma budhavākpatikāvyasauri
svarbhānuketu diviṣatpariṣatpradhānḥ |
tavaddāsadāsacaramāvadhidāsadāsāḥ
śrīveṅkaṭācalapate tava suprabhātam ||

Sūryaḥ (the Sun), Induḥ (the Moon), Bhaumaḥ (Mars), Budhaḥ (Mercury), Vākpatiḥ (Jupiter), Kavya (Venus), Sauriḥ (or śaniḥ-Saturn) Svarbhānuḥ (Rahu) and Ketuḥ (Ketu or comets) are the nine celestial bodies or Navagrahas which are the prominent ones in the assemblage of Divinities are the servants of the servants of your servants till the end of time.

Navagraha, or the nine planets (or celestial bodies), are important deities and many south Indian temples are not complete without a shrine to these.

Ancient Indians were especially fortunate in the variety of celestial bodies whose movements they could observe. Myths would have grown from such detailed notes of nature. Sections of the corpus of early

Indian literature contains observations of astronomical phenomena and nature, and current research has started helping us unpack the myths.[166]

Surya, the sun, is the son of Aditi and Kashyapa.[167] He rides a chariot whose horses are the seven poetic metres. Different sets of hermits and celestial beings ride on the sun's chariot every month and various combinations of these are responsible for heat, cold, rain, etc. Every day, at twilight, the sun has to battle with demons called the Mandehas who try to consume him but are eventually defeated and killed. This is echoed in the Egyptian legend of Ra's victory over Apophis every night. Yama is his son as is Karna from the Mahabharata.

Indu, or the moon god, is better known as Chandra. There is an interesting story about the waxing and waning of the moon. Chandra is married to the twenty-seven daughters of Daksha who are various stars. However, he was most fond of Rohini and spent most of his time with her. Due to this, his other twenty-six wives were unhappy and kept complaining. Despite their repeated requests, he ignored them. They went and complained to their father, but Chandra was in no mood to listen to his father-in-law, and due to Daksha's resultant curse, Chandra suffered from tuberculosis. Since he is the god of medicines too, medicinal plants stopped growing and, therefore, all living beings started suffering as a result. Since this state of affairs could not continue, a middle path was found so that the illness was halted for half a month, every month. Hence, the fifteen-day cycle of the moon.

Sukra, or Kavya, or the planet Venus, is the teacher of the asuras in Indian mythology.[168] The dictionary meanings of the word include white, pure, and bright.[169] (Even now, Venus stands brightest in the skies.) He is the teacher of Prahalada, who was rescued by the Narasimha avatara. In the Vamana avatara, when Lord Vishnu asked for three feet of earth from the demon king Mahabali, Sukracharya tried to intervene. At this, Lord Vishnu blinded him in one eye with a blade of grass.

Bhauma, or Mangal, is the planet Mars. The deity is said to have been born from the sweat of Lord Shiva and was nurtured by the earth goddess, Bhumi Devi in some versions. In others, he is said to have sprung from Bhumi Devi when she was a consort of the Varaha avatara. Since he is the son of Bhumi, his name is Bhauma.[170] The planet is also called Angaraka, Lohitanga, Raktavarna (all alluding to the red colour), Kuja or earth-born (seen in the morning before sunrise or in the evening after sunset, low on the horizon) and Bha or the one who shines. Due to its irregular movement, it is also called Vyala or Vakri. It would have been possible to name all of them based on their characteristics only because of detailed observation.

Buddha, or the planet Mercury, is said to be the son of the moon god and Tara, the wife of Brihaspati, or Jupiter. He married Ila and his son is the famous king, Pururavas. His chariot is made of wind and fire and is drawn by eight horses. Recent research into such phenomenon concludes that the ancient knew the type of movements that the planet made and mentioned that Mercury has seven types of movements.[171]

Vaakpati is Brihaspati, or the planet Jupiter, and is the teacher of gods. He is either one of the eight sons of the sage Angirasa, or of the fire god Agni, himself according to different versions. He has numerous wives and children in myth and one of his grandchildren is Dronacharya. Once, when Sukra, the teacher of demons, disappeared for a period of ten years, Brihaspati impersonated him with a view to wean the demons off their violent ways. As a consequence, they were cursed by their real teacher Sukra when he returned. In one of her births, Hanuman's mother was Sukra's servant and was cursed to become a monkey due to her inattentiveness.[172]

Sauri, or Shani (Saturn) is a revered figure in mythology. Many visit his temples on Saturday for wish fulfillment.

Svarbhanu, or Rahu, is eclipse in general and a villain of Indian mythology.[173] The myth is that his mother, Simhika, begged Kashyapa for a son when it was not appropriate and he cursed her with a dreadful son. After severe penance to Brahma, this son, Rahu, got boons that included the status of a planet, immortality, as well as the power to devour the sun and the moon. However, as he was rushing to fulfil his desire, Lord Vishnu cut off his head with his discus but let the proviso of the creator stand. Hence, Rahu causes both solar and lunar eclipses. The ancients knew eclipses very well and built a wide body of beliefs around them—for example, the sage Parasara was the first to mention the six-monthly cycle of lunar eclipses.[174]

Ketu is the name for all the comets. The formulation of Ketu being a node that is opposite Rahu is of a later origin—it is neither a lunar node nor is it a shadow. The earliest descriptions of Ketu are of celestial bodies which appear periodically and, apparently, many sages had expounded on this phenomenon; apart from Parashara, Asita, Devala, and Garga are mentioned as those who had studied comets.[175] Many texts refer to multiple Ketus or types of comets—the numbers range from 101 in some to 1,000 in another. There are three types of comets and they are said to assume many shapes.[176] The dictionary meaning has flag, banner, insignia, herald, and comet among others listed against the word and these may have been a tribute to its shape as well as its role as harbinger of events on earth.

❖

The work of collecting and cataloguing manuscripts and records continued with diligence till the middle of the previous century. What is worth highlighting, currently, is the continuing effort of the unsung folks who are on the frontline of safeguarding Indian heritage—the blue-collar staff who work in the manuscript repositories. They may be the worst paid among people who do such work in the world today, but are second to none in their dedication. Getting access is initially difficult but once the visitor's intention is ascertained, the help and support offered can be overwhelming. One such instance that I experienced was when the staff at the Sri Venkateswara University (SVU) Oriental research library decided to skip lunch to help me—I had a train to catch and was rushed for time. They brushed aside my thanks saying that requests for material such as mine came once in a decade and they looked forward to such occasions. Such encounters are the ultimate tonic in journeys like this.

As the corpus of manuscripts grew, a list of all available manuscripts in various collections became important, and in 1903, Theodor Aufrecht published his compendium of manuscripts mentioned in various catalogues and lists under the title *Catalogus Catalogorum*. But this work became outdated almost immediately as the enthusiasm for collecting manuscripts led to many manuscript repositories becoming known all over the country, and since many libraries vied to produce scholarly descriptive catalogues for easy reference, the available material became unmanageable. A.C. Woolner, the then vice chancellor of the Panjab University, proposed an overhaul of Aufrecht's work, and in 1935, the University of Madras took on the herculean task of bringing out an updated version.[177] This act of sustained scholarship has taken almost a century to finish and the completed set is called the *New Catalogus Catalogorum* (NCC).

Some of these manuscript collections are made accessible for the layperson by the descriptive catalogues of manuscripts which were being produced till a few decades ago. These catalogues were compiled by the leading scholars of the day, and in many of these, the descriptions provide a clear and informative precis of the manuscripts. The introductory notes in most of these catalogues are superb essays surveying the topic. The best catalogues are those of the Government Oriental Manuscripts Library (GOML), Chennai, which were printed around the time of independence, and of the Adyar Library and Research Centre in Chennai.

The NCC lists more than forty palm-leaf manuscripts of just the Venkateśa Suprabhātam.[178] Few other works dedicated exclusively to Lord Venkateswara have more manuscript copies—among those few, the *Venkatachala Mahatmayam* has been referred to in this book.[179] This manuscript corpus is large enough to highlight the enduring popularity of the suprabhātam genre as well as the widespread devotion to Lord Venkateswara in those centuries where other traces of the recitations are hard to find. It is also seen that some of the manuscripts of the four prayers composed by Anna got mixed up in other folios and works listed as other titles may actually be versions of the Venkateśa Suprabhātam or one of the three accompanying prayers.[180] A detailed examination of all the manuscript listings attributed to Anna in the NCC is the only way to pin down a number, and my guess is that it is going to be much more than forty. New additions to manuscript collections done in the last few decades which are not listed in the NCC may yield more copies.

These manuscripts are completely different from the sumptuously illustrated masterpieces of calligraphy that get the pride of place in most Indian manuscript collections. All of these are on plain, unadorned palm leaves, and time has taken a toll in most cases. These are not the indulgences of royalty but the aides-memoire for commoners. These would have been written for use of those who recite the prayer every day—some do not have the benedictory sentences like 'śrīveṅkaṭācalapate tava suprabhātam' and instead just note the first syllable of the benediction '*śrī*' as a cue to the reciter that he must repeat the complete benediction at this point. This also tells us that the users of such manuscripts would have been very familiar with the text and would know what to recite at which point.

The largest number of manuscripts of the Venkateśa Suprabhātam are written in the Grantha script which is close to the Tamil script. The handwriting varies and in many instances, reading the scrawled Grantha letters is a challenge—this also makes digital transliteration solutions more complex. Sentences in the manuscript may not be a straight line since most of the letters are inscribed with a nail-like implement. The Grantha script has changed very little over the last millennium (unlike say, old Kannada) and the scholars I consulted did not think textual analysis would help with the chronology.

The only indications of the date of the manuscripts given is provided by Oppert who indicates a possible time frame around the end of the eighteenth century for the four manuscripts that he collected, but since he relied on the memory of the manuscript owners, those dates need to be verified by experts. Since Grantha was prevalent in Tamil Nadu and southern Andhra Pradesh, it is safe for us to conclude that by this period, this prayer had moved out of the temple and had become a part of morning routines in households in the region in these periods.

Even those who worshipped other gods, had, by now, adopted the Venkateśa Suprabhātam as part of their morning recitation, and at least one manuscript seems to indicate that the Venkateśa Suprabhātam was by now recited as a general set of morning invocations.[181] This folio could have been the memory aid to the original owner for morning prayers to various deities.

१९

Tvatpādadhūli bharitasphuritottamāṅgāḥ
svargāpavarga nirapekṣanijāntaraṅgāḥ |
kalpāgamākalanayā kulatāṃ labhante
śrīveṅkaṭācalapate tava suprabhātam ||

The Lord's devotees including the divine beings have bathed in the dust of his feet and now stand purified and trembling. Since they are cloaked in his blessing, they look forward to the end of time indifferent to either heaven or salvation that may be their final state.

Since the verse talks about the dust beneath the feet of the Lord, it is useful to dwell for a while on the life of the saint Tondar Adi Poddi Azhvaar, whose ten-verse morning prayer to Lord Ranganatha of Srirangam may have inspired the Venkateśa Suprabhātam. His name literally means the 'dust beneath the feet of the devotees', and in Sanskrit, this Azhvaar is called 'Bhaktaanghrirenu', which means the same thing. The life of this Azhvaar is a tale of devotion, backsliding, and then redemption, which is why he is so easy to relate to in modern times.

He was born as Vipra Narayana in Tiru Mandanagudi near modern-day Kumbakonam. Piety came early, and even as a child, he was very devout and well-trained in the scriptures by his father. Once, he left Mandangudi on a pilgrimage and headed towards Srirangam. He seems to have been overcome by love for Lord Ranganatha—the form in which Vishnu is worshipped at Srirangam—and decided to stay there forever.

As a practical expression of devotion to his chosen god, Tondar Adi Podi Azhvaar cultivated a garden full of flowers and tulasi plants which were used for garlands for worship. He set up a small residence in the garden and looked all set for a life of piety and devotion to the lord.

In those days, there was a very famous pair of dancers called Devi and Devadevi. It seems Devadevi and her sister accidentally came to the garden. While resting, they saw the saint and were quite surprised by his immunity to their rather obvious charms. In a fit of pique, the sisters laid a wager on whether it was possible to seduce him. Devadevi got down to it and struck up an acquaintance with the saint. She offered to help in the garden and devoted herself to floriculture. Over time, the saint slowly descended from his exalted state of being and fell for the charms of the lady. He left the garden and went with Devadevi to her home, where he was not treated well. Soon Tondar Adi Podi Azhvaar was turned out of Devadevi's house and his degradation was now complete.

Lord Ranganatha decided to now intervene to rescue his man and an elaborate drama was played out. The lord manifested himself in the form of Azhvaar's servant, went to Devadevi's house, and gave her a golden vessel claiming that it belonged to the Azhvaar. The next day, the chief priest at the temple discovered that a golden chalice was missing from the temple and informed the king. A search of the town unearthed the said article in Devadevi's house. The authorities were informed that the vessel was handed over by the Azhvaar. The Azhvaar protested his poverty and his lack of domestic staff, but in vain.

Lord Ranganatha then appeared to the king in his dream and all was revealed. The Azhvaar, in his gratitude to the lord for showing him the error of his backsliding ways, decided to dedicate his life not just to the lord but also to the humble service of his devotees. He is therefore celebrated by all as 'one who is the dust beneath the feet of the devotees'. The attractive end to this tale is that Devadevi too joined him in the garden and helped him in his mission. He is said to have lived for a hundred and five years[182].

One wonders why God would subject a devotee like Tondar Adi Podi Azhvaar to such travails. Perhaps it was to trigger his inner creativity, as the Azhvaar then proceeded to compose two poems of outstanding beauty—one, the Tirumaalai, a forty-five-verse work, and the other, the above mentioned ten-verse Tirupalli Ezhuchi—which seems to have inspired Anna a few centuries later. While a fifty-five-verse corpus is a drop in the ocean that is the Four Thousand, their sheer devotional fervour and the life of the Azhvaar make them stand out.

❖

The largest repository of manuscripts of the Venkateśa Suprabhātam is in the GOML. The multi-volume descriptive catalogue of the GOML lists nine different manuscripts of the Venkateśa Suprabhātam. If the other three prayers—the Venkateśa Mangalasasanam, the Venkateśa Stotra, and the Venkateśa Prapatti—are also combined, there are twenty-seven manuscripts in the repository. If similar prayers to other 'main' deities, i.e., Vardaraja (Kanchipuram), Ranganatha (Srirangam), and

Yadavachalapati / Sampathkumara (Melkote) are added up, then the total corpus of laudatory prayers of this genre goes upto fifty-four manuscripts. Later catalogues of the GOML, like the Trennial Catalogue, have a few more listings.

Some of these have Anna's laudatory 'Taniyan' in the colophon. While the saint-composers believed that their composition was for the grace of god and not for personal aggrandisement, copies made by their followers would occasionally see the addition of a thaniyan or a laudatory verse of the saint / poet as a colophon.

The Adyar Library and Research Centre of the Theosophical Society in Chennai too has a superb collection of manuscripts. While its descriptive catalogues are not as detailed as those of GOML, the introductory notes are superb—reading them is like attending a lecture on that particular genre. The Library has six manuscripts of the Venkateśa Suprabhātam and twenty-two manuscripts of the four poems combined.

The SVU Oriental Research Institute at Tirupati has a few manuscripts of the Venkateśa Suprabhātam, as does the Oriental Research Library at Mysore. There are a few in Ecole Francaise and as seen earlier, Oppert mentions four copies in his catalogue. Mackenzie must have also collected a copy, but that is not yet certain.

The Trennial Catalogue of the GOML is a catalogue of manuscripts collected in the 1930s by the Madras Library. It describes a couple of curiosities related to the Suprabhātam. One is a manuscript called the Venkatesadayita Suprabhātam—a morning prayer dedicated to the consort of Sri Venkateswara, the goddess Alamelu Manga. It also lists a manuscript of a Venkateśa Suprabhātam composed by a certain Sudarsana of

Vadhula Gotra.[183] Going by the beginning and the endings described in the catalogue, this is an original composition by itself. It seems a more difficult text and this version is known from only one manuscript. Still, the very existence of this one manuscript is evidence that a few centuries after its composition, the Venkateśa Suprabhātam was popular enough to spawn imitations in Sanskrit in addition to the vernacular composition by Pedda Tirumalacharya.

Apart from the suprabhātam to Lord Venkateswara, these manuscript libraries have many versions of suprabhātams to different manifestations of Vishnu as well as to other gods. The morning prayers to manifestations of Vishnu worshipped as Vardaraja (at Kanchipuram), Yadavachalpati (at Melkote), and Ranganatha (at Srirangam) abound. This itself speaks of the popularity of the genre in the period, and given that the Venkateśa Suprabhātam was probably the first, its appeal and impact can be best gauged by this profusion. Some of the other suprabhātams also carry Anna's thaniyan and support the claim that he composed a suprabhātam for each of the 108 holy places.[184]

२०

tvadgopurāgraśikharāṇi nirīkṣamāṇāḥ
svargāpavargapadavīṃ paramāṃ śrayantaḥ |
martyā manuṣyabhuvane matimāśrayante
śrīveṅkaṭācalapate tava suprabhātam ||

Just the sight of the tops of the soaring spires of your abode makes even those mortals who have attained salvation stay back in this world. Arise, O Lord of Venkatachala.

The soaring spires can also be the lofty peaks of Tirumala, and thus this verse implies that even looking up at Tirumala from the plains below is enough to make the devotees feel that they have attained salvation.

The soaring spires of Tirumala are just one part of the extraordinary architectural treasures of the temple. However, anyone interested in the architecture of the Tirumala temple nowadays will find it very difficult to experience it first-hand. After being made to stay in the queue complex for a few hours and then being part of the press of devotees for the next half an hour as it surges towards the sanctum sanctorum, all are only focused on reaching in front of Lord Venkateswara and digressions are near impossible.

Fortunately, many aspects of the Tirumala temple have been studied for almost a century by some of the greatest scholars of the time, and one of them, S.K. Ramachandra Rao, introduces his work with the following words: 'The movement of the queue lines precludes his (i.e. the pilgrim's) having a look at the structural details … and he can have no idea whatever of the … architecture of the temple.' After agreeing that folks who would be interested in such minutiae will be a small minority, he goes on to add: 'It is for these few that my book has been planned. I have attempted to provide here as graphic a description of the various structural details …'[185] This book, *The Hill-Shrine of Vengadam* (here onward *The Hill-Shrine*) is an extraordinary work and, in some ways, an inspiration for the current work. Like this book, *The Hill-Shrine* follows a poem, called the 'Sri Venkateśa Seva Krama' (VSK) that traces the walk of a pilgrim from the bottom of the hill to the temple till the pilgrim reaches the main idol. It is also one of the few eyewitness accounts of a pilgrimage to Tirumala in the centuries past, and by retracing the walk in *The Hill-Shrine,* S.K. Ramachandra Rao has set the bar very high for 'past and present' accounts.

Out of the plethora of architectural details that *The Hill-Shrine* describes, I saw only a few. The first feature that one notices on the climb up is also the first of the 'spires and towers' of the Tirumala temple which is the Alipiri Manadapam at the foothills. This is the starting point for the walk up to Tirumala—Alipiri means the lowest step in the stairway.[186] Even at 4 a.m. in the morning, there is a crowd as early birds throng the walkway. Ramachandra Rao talks about the gopuram surmounting the mandapam, but I missed it. There are numbered steps to the top of the hill, and apart from a few sections in the beginning and towards the latter part, the walk itself is not very taxing.

The Gali Gopuram comes as a welcome relief after a steep initial ascent. As mentioned elsewhere, this was constructed by Kumara Anataraja of the Matla family. Nowadays, those who walk up are allotted an expected time of entry into the temple queue complex at this point. According to the VSK, there are excellent views through the climb and one could pause and see the valley spread below. The poem describes the lakes, tanks, gardens, the river Suvarnamukhi, the temple of Govindaraja, and the other sights of Sripuri town, i.e., Tirupati from this and other vantage points,[187] and all these sights could still be seen from the pathway till a few decades ago.

The temple to Ramanuja suddenly emerges on the pathway. It is a small, quiet, and a well-maintained shrine. Those who wish to can spend a few peaceful moments here. This shrine also marks the beginning of the holy area of Venkata Hill.[188]

Along the way, there is a small and very old shrine to Yoga Narasimha.

Statues of each of the Azhvaars begin from sometime around this stage in the walk. Each statue is accompanied by a small write-up which includes a brief bio of the Azhvaar and the number of verses that each composed on the Tirumala temple. It is very informative and the statues themselves are very attractive.

Some of the features along the walkway mentioned in the VSK were either dilapidated or removed by the time Ramachandra Rao wrote his book, and in 2019, completely escaped attention. By now, the pilgrim path reaches Tirumala and according to the VSK and also Ramachandra Rao, the main golden dome (vimana)of the temple called Ananda Nilaya would have been visible in the past.[189] This is a distinctive feature and one we see in all pictures of the temple. In Anna's time, in the early fifteenth-century, this dome would have been even more pervasive and would have visually dominated the landscape—the 'soaring spires' could not have been missed by any. It can no longer be seen from the place where the covered walkway from Alipiri enters the main concourse in Tirumala.

The Varahaswami Temple is a small and ancient temple to the Varaha avatara which is located on the far side of the Pushkarini tank (which has been described elsewhere). It is customary that a visit to this temple precedes a visit to Lord Venkateswara—few follow this practice nowadays and hence queues here are shorter.

The 'writing on the wall' on stones on the outer walls of the temple is an interesting detail that Ramachandra Rao dwells upon.[190] The stones were marked with characters from chants so that the masons who were building the wall would know how to place them in the desired sequence. These numbered stones can now be seen as the pilgrim is borne in the queue along the walls after coming out of the Vaikuntam queue complex. It is an exhilarating moment when, in the middle of the crush, one finds a quiet second to observe a character on the stone (you have to look over your left shoulder when you are next to the wall to see these) and realise that one is standing at the same spot that the nameless masons and workers who built the temple would have stood and toiled in the centuries past.

The Mahadwara, or the main door, which is described in loving detail by Rao, passes in a blur.

There are courtyards and passageways around the shrine but the modern pilgrim is unable to get a sense of these as the queue has a life of its own and surges towards the lord. From this point onward, whatever one can see inside the temple are just momentary vignettes. Inside, the temple is exquisitely beautiful, and while the press of pilgrims may seem to overwhelm, there is still so much to appreciate.

On one side is the Ayana Mahal, or Hall of Mirrors. Rao tells us that this is where the famous Tirupati ladoos used to be kept in the past.[191]

After this, one passes through the inner door into an open space. This is the Vimana Pradakshina and this passage surrounds the main shrine. The entire space is visually dominated by gilded doors and enclosures of the main shrine. Beyond this point, devotees cannot notice the architectural details. The queue leads through one side into the temple and, before one realises, one is turning into the final stretch in front of the main idol of Lord Venkateswara. There is a slight rise here as the queue turns left into the sanctum sanctorum and those who can somehow pause here will get their first sight of Lord Venkateswara.

On the way out, there is the Sankirtana Bhandagaram on the side where Tallapaka Annamacharya's descendants collected their songs.[192]

I wanted to see the Ranga Mandapam which housed the statue of Lord Ranganatha for some decades in the fourteenth century and where Anna would have been instructed to compose the Venkateśa Suprabhātam. Spending a quiet ten minutes in front of this mandapam would have been the culmination of my journey. However, that was not to be—the staff were too busy managing the crowds to give more than cursory directions, and in the general rush, it is difficult to find anything other than the exit.

The statues of various grandees are arranged in backlit cabinets on either side of the doorway and Krishna Deva Raya and his queens take pride of place. The statue of Lala Khema Ram aka Todar Malla can also be seen along with those of his wife and mother. There is also a statue of Venkatapati Raya, but I missed it.

Ours is a living history and even today, we stand where the greatest of saints and kings would have stood in the centuries gone by and experience what millions of ordinary folk would have felt.

❖

Sadatullah Khan became the Nawab of Carnatic in 1713 after some decades of turbulence and brought much-needed peace to the region. The Venkateswara temple found a benefactor in his minister, Todar Malla, who managed to perpetuate the fact of his devotion at Tirumala by having statues of himself and his wife and mother installed inside the temple as mentioned above.[193] Todar Malla or Lala Khema Ram had already burnished his credentials as a devotee of Vishnu with his services to the Kanchipuram temple, and perhaps it was his influence which allowed the Tirumala temple to sail serenely through this period of general strife.

Sadatullah Khan was succeeded by his nephew Dost Ali who kept the peace till his death in 1740 while confronting a Maratha expedition. Nawab Dost Ali's passing inaugurated a general free-for-all which is now referred to as the Carnatic Wars. When the dust finally settled in 1763, the English were the masters of the field and had secured another toehold in India (after Bengal in 1757).

During this period, the list of people who have toiled through the ages to serve Lord Venkateswara became more diverse when, in 1753, the East India Company teamed up with the then nawab of Carnatic's brother, Najibullah Khan, to defend Tirumala against the adventurer Mohammed Kamal. Ensign Holt, who commanded the English detachment, died in action. Robert Orme stirringly describes the episode, which ends with the peremptory beheading of Md Kamal by N. Khan.[194] In turn, a few years later, the temple had to be protected from the attentions of Najibullah Khan.

In 1751, around a decade before the Carnatic Wars finally ended, the nawab of Carnatic had been forced to hand over the revenues of Tirumala to the English and they started receiving an annual rent of more than 50,000 pagodas.[195] Given its importance as a source of steady funds, others tried to wrest it away from the English, notably the French and the Marathas, but though nominally Tirupati and Tirumala belonged to the Nawab of Carnatic, the East India Company managed to hang on to the revenue.

It is estimated that the English were extracting two and half lakh rupees annually from Tirupati in the period.[196] Since the English colonial project in India started in right earnest from this part of India in 1763, this steady annuity may have been key in enabling the English to first beat back the French, then resist the terminal threat posed by Hyder Ali,[197] and finally, take the first steps to subcontinental domination. Even before the Battle of Plassey, the English had found durable means to further their colonial project when the rent of Lord Venkateswara's temple at Tirumala was assigned to them in 1751.[198]

By the end of the eighteenth century, the English had defeated all their other competitors for political power in South India and had hence concluded that the nawabs of Carnatic were of no further use to them. The last nawab settled for a pension, the East India Company took over the direct administration of his territory, attached the Tirumala temple to the North

Arcot district and appointed George Stratton collector for the area (the 'Western Poliams', as they were called) in 1801.

Though he himself did not actually visit the temple, Stratton made a detailed account of the practices in force. There is an inevitable revenue estimate, among other things. To prepare his report, he instituted an enquiry to capture the practices and beliefs that were prevalent in the temple at that point. He verified the details, and on the basis of what he learnt, Stratton published his famous report on the Tirumala temple.[199]

One of the key components of this exhaustive survey took the form of a detailed questionnaire which sought answers to some key questions. The answers were finally codified in the following documents—the Sawal-e-Jawab Patti, the Kainkarya Patti, the Paimayashi Patti and the Dittam book.[200] Some parts of the Sawal-e-Jawab Patti were published by the Mythic Society in Bengaluru in the late 1940s.

These records have been seen and studied by generations of administrators subsequently. N. Ramesan, who as one-time executive officer of the TTD would have had access to every record of the temple, uses the contents of the Sawal-e-Jawab Patti extensively in his book on the temple.

It is in one of the sections of the Sawal-e-Jawab Patti that we find the first record of the recitation of the Venkateśa Suprabhātam in three centuries. In the reply to a question about the designation and names of various people who served the temple, it was stated that descendants of Tallapaka Annamacharya recited the Suprabhātam in the morning after the main door of the sanctum was opened—as of 1819, the Venkateśa Suprabhātam was being recited in front of Lord Venkateswara, and members of the Tallapaka family were reciting it.[201]

Given S. Subramania Sastri's surmise that Pedda Tirumalacharya was given a share of the offering for reciting the Suprabhātam in the mid-sixteenth century then it seems that for the intervening centuries, the descendants of the saint Annamacharya were reciting the morning prayer in front of Lord Venkateswara regularly.

Three centuries of steadfast adherence to the routine of reciting a prayer which was composed by another saint, in uncertain and difficult times and while possibly enduring personal hardships is an inspirational tale of devotion, both to the almighty and to duty. While it is easy to be devout when the environment is favourable, the truly faithful make it count when times are tough. The Tallapakas are owed a debt of gratitude for this service, which has continued in recent times.[202]

२१

śrībhūmināyakadayādiguṇāmṛtābdhe
devādhideva jagadekaśaraṇyamūrte |
śrīmannananta garuḍādibhirarcitāṅghre
śrīveṅkaṭācalapate tava suprabhātam ||

O guide of the world, O ocean of virtues like mercy, O Lord of the Gods, O sole protector of the world, O one whose feet are forever worshipped by the likes of Garuda, O Lord of Venkatachala, arise.

Vaishnavism believes that God should be conceivable so that people can love him and more importantly, try to emulate his qualities. Qualities which are needed in everyday life are a lot easier to attain and a personification of these will motivate people to emulate them.

Vishnu has many manifestations and many classes of manifestations through which he and his qualities may be known. These are called the avataras.[203]

An important question is, why does a divinity who was anyway all-pervasive need specific manifestations?

In the Bhagavad Gita, the Sri Krishna avatara provides specific answers to why and when manifestations occur. Manifestations happen when the correct path decays and the incorrect path prospers. Further, their objective is to protect the good, destroy wrongdoers, and reestablish the correct path in every age. The manifestations are not for the exaltation of God but for the relief of his creation. He takes a recognisable form out of kindness since the majority of creation may not be capable of comprehending a formless all-pervasive supreme force.

Vishnu manifests himself for the benefit of mankind in the following ways according to the Sri Vaishnava system—Para, Vyuha, Vibhava, Arca, and Antaryami.[204]

The Para form is the primordial eternal form of Vishnu. The Vyuha forms are manifestations of his qualities. The Vibhava avatara are manifestations in the forms of heroes or supreme beings for the benefit of mankind. The Arca avataras are the idols and statutes which are imbued with divinity and are easily accessible to all. The final form, or the Antaryami form, is the god within each and every being.

The distinction between these manifestations is explained with simple analogies by Pillai Lokacharya, one of the greatest teachers of the system post Ramanujacharya. According to him, the Para form is like water in the atmosphere surrounding the material universe, the Vyuha is like the ocean, and the Vibhava is like flash floods in rivers when the monsoon comes—they benefit those who are present at the right place at the right time. The Arca avatara is like the still water in ponds and water bodies—it is easily accessible to everyone who is needy, and finally, the Antaryami is like the ground water deep below the surface—one has to work hard to reach it.[205] Understanding difficult metaphysical concepts becomes easy through such analogies of nature and everyday life.

The Para form is the transcendental, eternal, all-pervasive form which is found in Vaikunta. This all-pervasive force is beyond human conception. This manifestation is sometimes referred to as Para Vasudeva.

This transcendental form is the source of all the other classes of manifestations and sub-manifestations. An earlier work on the topic describes this form: 'The Divine Figure is adorned with nine chief ornaments and weapons, which symbolically represent the principles of the universe, namely, the Kaustubha (a jewel worn on the breast) = the souls, the Srivatsa (a curl of hair on the breast)= Prakrti, a club = Mahat, a conch = the Sattvic Ahamkara, a bow = the Tamasic Ahamkara, a sword = knowledge, its sheath = ignorance, the discus = the mind, the arrows = the senses, a garland = the Elements. These weapons and ornaments are not merely regarded as symbols but also as actually connected (as presiding deities or the like) with the Tattvas (elements) they represent.'[206]

This manifestation possesses the six principal attributes—Jnana (omniscience), Shakti (omipotence), Bala (the quality of upholding creation without effort), Aisvarya (lordship / ownership of all actions), Virya (the ability to remain undecaying), Tejas (splendour and self-sufficiency).[207] Though the god's qualities are infinite, Ramanujacharya and other teachers have highlighted the attributes encompassing all the qualities of compassion, tenderness, empathy, good fellowship, and peacefulness that Lord Vishnu is known and loved for.[208]

When Anna sings about the ocean of all virtues like kindness, this is what he means.

❖

Meanwhile, far away from Tirumala, in north India, and long before this period, the saint Ramananda had accepted Sri Ramachandra as the ultimate reality. His work and that of his twelve disciples—of whom Kabir is the most famous—recrafted the spiritual landscape of the north in the next few centuries. Swamy Ramananda's work and that of his disciples needs to be understood, even today, as an unending effort to keep the worship of Vishnu—in his incarnation as Sri Ramachandra—non-sectarian and inclusive.

The Bairagi sanyasis follow this tradition and one of them came to Tirumala some centuries ago and built a hermitage near the temple. The lord himself blessed him with a vision and started coming for a daily game of dice with him. The most famous tale of a miracle associated with this saint recounts how Lord Venkateswara took the form of a wild elephant to help the saint consume a room full of sugarcane overnight (hence his name—

Swamy Hathiram Bawaji).[209] A matha was established in his name and as the worship of Lord Venkateswara spread, this matha and its mahants started playing a key role in organising pilgrimages from different parts of the country to Tirumala.[210] As political conditions deteriorated and the situation in the Deccan became unstable, these wandering ascetics provided much-needed protection to the pilgrim bands and became the face of the temple in many parts of India.

By the middle of the nineteenth century, the mahants of the Hathiram Matha had gained an important place in the affairs of the Tirumala temple, and their influence rivalled that of the Jiyars—the descendants of the various teachers appointed by Ramanujacharya as well as the hereditary Vaikhanasa priestly families. To put things in perspective, in 1801, the Hathiram Matha held 9,225 guntas of inam land (land given as compensation for service) as against the 13,091 guntas held by all other functionaries, pontiffs, hereditary teachers, and priestly families put together. At the same time, the Prativadi Bhayankaram and the Tallapaka families held 561 guntas and 1,600 guntas of inam lands respectively.[211]

As the English took over parts of India, they also appropriated the revenues from various religious institutions. As time passed, the East India Company's administration of Indian religious institutions came under attack for what was considered unsolicited meddling in the internal affairs of indigenous institutions. Presciently, in light of what happened in 1857, the powers that be at Fort St George recalled Thomas Munro's note at the time of the Vellore mutiny of 1806 which suggested that continued interference in ancient laws and customs of the land will cause widespread disaffection. Hence, Lord Auckland, the Governor General of India from 1836 to 1842, decided to relinquish control of the Tirumala temple, among other religious institutions, and hand them back to an Indian administration.

When the English decided to hand the Tirumala temple back to the Indians, the ascetics of the Hathiram Matha emerged as front-runners for taking over the administration. After some to-ing and fro-ing among the various interested parties, in 1843, the management of the Tirumala temple was handed over to the then mahant. He and his five successors were called the Vicharanakartas and they administered the temple from 1843 to 1933. Their administration was dogged by a string of litigations, and the tenure of the first Vicharankarta—Mahant Sevadossji (1843—1864)—was the only time in this phase of its history that the temple's matters were not in the courts.[212]

The Vicharankartas introduced innovations like the first telephone line to Tirumala, while at the same time refurbishing the temple and reinstated traditional usages. One of their innovations could have possibly impacted the recitation of the Venkateśa Suprabhātam, as in 1844, the first Vicharankarta is said to have restricted the Tallapaka family from singing inside the temple.[213] This decision must have been rescinded as the Suprabhātam continued to be recited.

Printed copies of the prayer started appearing regularly soon after. The oldest seems to be a version printed by the Sarasvati Nilaya Press in Telugu script in 1868, followed by another in 1870 in Grantha script by the Hindubhashasanjivini Press. The Sarasvati Nilaya Press brought out two more editions in 1875 and 1881.[214]

A railway line from Nellore reached Tirupati in 1887, and by 1907, the third-class fare from Madras Beach Junction to Tirupati was Rs 3 and 8 annas for a Boat Mail train, and Rs 3 for other trains.[215] The great pilgrim onrush to Tirumala had started in right earnest by the turn of the twentieth century. While there would have been places to stay in Tirumala in earlier times, by the first decade of the new century, a hospital, a choultry (rest house), water facilities, and a road were all sanctioned for the journey up to the holy hill. [216] The Grantha script versions of the prayer were still being printed in 1917, and by 1924, printing presses in distant Bombay were including the Venkateśa Suprabhātam in their prayer-book editions.

The last Vicharankarta, Mahant Prayag Dossji assumed the 'gaddi' (seat) in 1900 at a young age. He was energetic and started many initiatives. The work of recording all the inscriptions found in the temples at Tirumala and Tirupati started in his tenure. By the 1920s, as efforts intensified to replace the Vicharankartas, the scene of dispute shifted from the courts to the legislature. Mahant Prayag Dossji fought till the end and the pages of the scholarly journal that he had started to research aspects of the temple, Tirumalai Sri Venkateswara, are full of appeals and petitions to the English in Madras, Delhi, Shimla, and London to stop the transfer of administration.

Tucked away in a back page of the journal of the early 1930s, after chapters of petitions and impassioned outpourings in favour of the Vicharankartas, we find advertisements for various publications of prayer books and other such religious compositions. The Venkateśa Suprabhātam is listed here. It was available for sale both in the Telugu script (for 2 annas) and in the Devanagari script (for 4 annas). Apparently, in the middle of juggling administrative tasks and multiple legal issues, as well as lobbying hard with the government, Mahant Prayag Dossji had still found time to commission an early 'official' printed version of the Venkateśa Suprabhātam.

Such a succession of editions in multiple languages for more than fifty years means that prayer books containing the Venkateśa Suprabhātam would have been in homes across south India by the first quarter of the twentieth century. Much before independence, the prayer seems to have been very popular for a recitation of what was, even then, a semi-secret morning ritual.

Soon after, the TTD formally took over the administration of Tirumala in 1933 after the government passed the Tirumalai Tirupati Devasthanam Act of 1932.

The recitation of Venkateśa Suprabhātam would have continued as a private morning ritual before the general public was allowed in. In 1943, TTD's scholars published a collection of previously published and unpublished prayers in praise of Lord Venkateswara called the *Sri Venkateśa Kavya Kalapa*. The Venkateśa Suprabhātam leads the collection. The poem is introduced as a gift of 'Vadibheekaraguru'—an epithet for Anna .

By publishing the temple version of all the famous prayers and prayers, TTD also rendered a great service to future generations by establishing a 'standard' version from the various manuscripts, and subsequent recitations adhere to this version of the Venkateśa Suprabhātam.

|| SECTION FOUR ||

By the time India became independent, the Tirumala temple had regained its glory under the energetic management of the Tirumala Tirupati Devasthanams (TTD). Gandhiji loved the songs of the Vaishnava devotional saints;[217] the Meera Bhajans of M.S. Subbulakshmi were a particular favourite and she was to play a pivotal role in the popularity of this prayer. From the middle of the century, the growth of different broadcasting media helped in finding new ways for the spread of devotional material, and through TV serials in the late 1980s, newer generations rediscovered the avataras of Lord Vishnu.

The Venkateśa Suprabhātam is one of the biggest beneficiaries of improvements in mass broadcasting in modern India, and the popularity of the prayer in present times owes a lot to its adaptability to various media. The gramophone recording of the prayer created the genre of devotional music recordings and drew many new listeners to nascent radio broadcasts of the newly independent country, both for its devotional message as well as for an introduction to the world of Carnatic music.

These innovations and the genius of M.S. Subbulakshmi combined to make this fifteenth century composition a twentieth-century phenomenon. Also, this combination of the prayer, technology, and musical genius unwittingly gave an intangible boost to Carnatic music in general.

As the twenty first century progresses, the Venkateṣa Suprabhātam continues to permeate the morning landscape in south India, and elevates and inspires new listeners even today. The popularity of this prayer and the attendant service at Tirumala can be gauged by the attendance to the service through the decades. Around the time of independence, it was still a quiet semi-private service, and those devotees who were able to reach when the doors were open wọuld wait and listen. As the decades progressed, more and more wanted to hear the recitation and prioritisation was needed. Initially, those who offered an Angapradakshina service were allowed first. The popularity kept increasing and it then became a paid service. Nowadays, the demand is such that devotees who can participate in this service are selected through a lottery system.

२२

śrīpadmanābha puruṣottama vāsudeva
vaikuṇṭhamādhava janārdana cakrapāṇe |
śrīvatsacihna śaraṇāgatapārijāta
śrīveṅkaṭācalapate tava suprabhātam ||

One who has a lotus in the navel, O most superior among those with Individual souls, O son of

> ***Vasudeva, One who is the remover of obstacles (to liberation), O one with the discus in his hand, O one who kills those who are antagonistic to his devotees, O Lord of Lakshmi, One with the auspicious Srivatsa mark on his chest,[218] O divine tree which forever protects his devotees, Good morning to you.***

The many names of Vishnu are mentioned here. These are a few of the thousand names of Lord Vishnu that are enshrined in the popular prayer, Vishnu Sahasranama.

The next class of manifestations is called the Vyuha. The transcendental Para form splits into four Vyuha forms; namely, Vasudeva, Sankarsana, Pradyumna, and Anirudha. As seen earlier, Lord Vishnu is defined by six principal qualities; namely, jnana (awareness), bala (strength), sakti (power), aisvarya (overlordship/ independence), virya (energy), and tejas (splendour). Vyuha avatara is the manifestation of these attributes and may be thought of as a special purpose vehicle to disseminate his qualities.

The Vasudeva Vyuha form possesses all six. The next three—Sankarsana, Pradyumna, and Aniruddha—are named after the brother, son, and grandson of Krishna and show the extent to which the system was derived from the worship of Vasudeva Krishna. Each of these three other Vyuhas is Vishnu himself with his six qualities, of which, in each case, two are prominent.

The three Vyuhas—Sankarsana, Pradyumna, and Anirudha—have creative as well as moral roles. From each Vyuha descend three subordinate Vyuha avataras. Saṅkarsana begets Govinda, Vishnu, and Madhusudana; Pradyumna reincarnates as Trivikrama, Vamana, and

Sridhara; and Aniruddha as Hrisikesa, Padmanabha, and Damodara.[219]

❖

After the First World War ended, the post-war radio boom reached Indian shores in the 1920s. Radio broadcasting in India owes a lot to the initial efforts of the Radio Clubs of Bombay, Calcutta and Madras that started in 1923-24. The government started the Indian Broadcasting Service in 1930 and appointed Lionel Fielden as controller of broadcasting in 1935. The various princely states too jumped in and the Mysore State heard radio broadcasts under the name 'Akashvani' in 1935. The network run by the British government was formally renamed All India Radio in 1936.

By the dawn of independence, radio listening was part of the daily life of many, and in August 1947, Mountbatten, Pandit Nehru, and M.A. Jinnah all made their historic broadcasts on AIR. Post-independence, the Delhi, Calcutta, Madras, Bombay, Lucknow, and Trichy stations stayed with India, and the Lahore, Peshawar, and Dacca stations went to Pakistan. The process of merging the networks of princely states and other stations continued till 1954.[220]

A few years before this, an unknown trend spotter in HMV, who must have been a frequent visitor to the shrine at Tirumala, sensed that the Venkateśa Suprabhātam had the power to inspire millions. Armed with this inexplicable foresight about what was still a private ritual, HMV decided that the time was right for a long-playing record (LP) of the prayer. They requested TTD to nominate the best person to do this recording, and at the behest of the then executive officer of TTD, Sri C. Anna Rao, Sri P.V. Ananthasayanam Iyengar (the Vedaparayana Karta or Vedic Reciter) in Tirumala agreed to do a recording. A box set of four LPs was released soon and this rare recording is probably the first ever of the Venkateśa Suprabhātam.[221] Saregama, the current right-holders to that original version, published it on YouTube in 2014. Apparently, AIR released a recording in 1979, but this recitational gem remains unknown. Even now, years after its publication on the internet, this recording has garnered very few views.

Listening to Ananthasayanam Iyengar's recording is a completely different experience from listening to the popular recitation of the Venkateśa Suprabhātam (i.e., MS's recording). Since few other prayers of such current popularity have been recorded while being recited by the traditional reciters, this recording is a tiny gem in the cultural heritage of southern India. The recitation is mellow, has a slow pace, and it is likely to be the closest to what must have been recited through the centuries. Recitational nuances are best understood by listening to this as it is a slower recitation and its playing time is longer than that of MS's version.

The life of P.V. Ananthasayanam Iyengar is one of the 'small' histories, whose pursuit has made this journey so fulfilling. It was difficult, as his sons were not easy to locate,[222] and such is his influence on them even forty years after his death that they were initially reticent to speak about him.

He was born outside Kanchipuram and was trained in the Vedas and their recitation by his father, Krishnamachariar. Ananthasayanam Iyengar worked for eighteen years at the temple at Tiruvahindrapuram near Cuddalore. His early years were very difficult and the family had to face a lot of hardship.

His recitational fluency brought him the recognition and friendship of P.B. Anangaracharya of Kanchipuram, one of the original Anna's descendants who was a famous religious teacher of the twentieth century. Ananthasayanam Iyengar started his service as a vedic reciter in the Tirumala temple in the early 1950s. Unlike many in those days, he did not have hereditary rights to such services but was selected due to his fluency and skill. Apart from the Venkateśa Suprabhātam, Iyengar also recited the Vishnu Sahasranamam and various other prayers daily. He was assisted by a team of twelve, and for almost three decades—till the late 1970s—he was the daily face of recitations at the temple.

P.V. Ananthasayanam Iyengar became the defining image of the recitation at the temple and his is the male voice of the Venkateśa Suprabhātam. He was assisted in his live recitations by T.E. Sundaravarada Thathachariar, whom he held in high esteem. However, in his HMV recording of the Suprabhātam, there is a shadow female voice. According to his son, that is the voice of the young daughter of one of HMV's employees who was trained by Iyengar. That unnamed lady, who would now be in her eighties (if she is still alive), would thus be the first female public broadcaster of the Venkateśa Suprabhātam. Iyengar handed over the royalty rights of his recitation to the temple, soon after its release.

By the mid-1950s, the TTD decided to make a documentary called the 'Venkateswara Vaibhavam' about the rituals and ceremonies at Tirumala. The voice-over of all the prayers in the documentary is that of Ananthasayanam Iyengar. Since sections of this documentary were shot in Madras, the TTD deputed him to teach the prayer to M.S. Subbulakshmi; his eldest son has vivid memories of accompanying his father to MS's home in Kalki Gardens during this period.

Iyengar's approach to the daily service of reciting the Venkateśa Suprabhātam is best summed up in his own words in a newspaper article that came out shortly after his tenure in Tirumala was extended in 1976. He said, 'Sound like god is without form and self-created and is the beginning. Sound reaches out to the one who is listening all the time. My job is beyond the fault-finding audit and yet I dare not commit an error in diction, nuance or stress as I believe more than the human ear's listening.' He added, 'I have nothing to do with men who run the temple, officials, VIPs or the devout. And the marvellous thing is that there is no routine or familiarity: every morning is a new one for me and I am filled with wonder.' [223] His son thinks his father could not live away from Lord Venkateswara. Shortly after his service ended at Tirumala, Iyengar died of a stroke in Pondicherry in 1979. A life and a voice spent entirely in service without any fanfare or expectation of reward.

२३

Kandarpadarpaharasundara divyamūrte
kāntā kucāmburuha kuḍmalaloladṛṣṭe |
kalyāṇanirmalaguṇākara divyakīrte
śrīveṅkaṭācalapate tava suprabhātam ||

> ***Your form is such that even Kama, the god of Love is humbled by it. Your gaze constantly seeks the beauteous form of your beloved. Your countenance is pure, virtuous, divine and its glimpse bestows salvation on the beholder.***

This verse can mean 'beauty to surpass Kama' and also 'form which will make all beings impervious to the power of Kama'. It deals with the beautiful form of God and may be a description of the idol of god.

God or the Supreme Force extolled in the Vedas is formless and beyond human comprehension. The Agamas follow this position. The only sure way to approach such a formless concept is through meditation and inner journey. The Agamas therefore always prescribe yoga (discipline and practice) for physical and mental control, and therefore as a method to seek the ultimate reality.

However, as society evolved, such formulations became too abstract for the general public and the need was felt for more relatable concepts for people to worship. While the Vibhava avatara gave the Godhead a relatable shape, it could only help those who lived at the same time as that specific manifestation. You had to exist at the time the manifestation took place to get the benefit.

Hence, there is conception of the Arca avatara which is an easy path available to most of mankind. It is believed that, in many instances, god may imbue an idol or a totem with divine qualities. Once consecrated, these idols/statues may be worshipped as a manifestation of Vishnu himself. The manifestations enjoy varying degrees of devotion. A few are very popular and

Tirumala is the foremost among them. Most other locations/manifestations are less sought after but seem to have an equal ability to quieten the soul.

By worshipping the idol, the devotee too gains a little bit of those divine qualities as this is a conception that does not require any qualification or condition. Idol worship therefore represented an important step in making spirituality more accessible to common people.

The Vaikhanasa Agama mentions five types of idols, or 'bera', in temples. These are called Dhruva Bera, Kautuka Bera, Snapana Bera, Utsava Bera, and Bali Bera. The Dhruva Bera, also called Mula Bera or Moolavar, is the main idol of the god being worshipped—in Tirumala, it is Lord Venkateswara. This idol can never be disturbed from its position once it is consecrated. The Dhruva Bera may be standing, sitting, or lying down. Often, the Dhruva Beras are gigantic and immovable. The need was felt for a surrogate for devotees to offer prayers or perform rituals. Kautuka Bera is often the mobile version of the Dhruva Bera and worship is offered to both. As festivals started taking place in temples, and also for the convenience of those who were too sick or otherwise unable to come to the temple, the need was felt for a statue which could be taken out in processions. This is called the Utsava Bera. There was also a need for a ceremonial bath daily. Idols that are largely used for this purpose are called Snapana Bera. Finally, there is the Bali Bera, to which offerings can be made.[224]

The Dhurva Bera in Tirumala of Lord Venkateswara is self-manifested and it is believed that it has not been created by any human. The idol is in a standing position and is said to be close to eight feet tall. Describing this form is difficult and, in the words of one writer, '... is experienced but not perceived, felt but not caught; it is an encounter that is at once satisfying, but leaves one yearning for more of it. It is full of spiritual power and, therefore, not to be approached by all people'.[225]

As more and more devotees flocked to the temple, there was a need for more offerings to Lord Venkateswara. The Kautuka Bera, which is a smaller silver copy of the main idol, was consecrated in 966 CE (according to some authorities; others posit 614 CE as the year of consecration).[226] This was called Manvallaperumal and is now generally known as Bhoga Srinivasa.

The Utsava Bera, or the processional idol, is called Malayappan, which is a short form for Malai Kuniya Ninra Perumal, and the first mention of this idol is in an inscription dated 1339 CE.[227] The idol is about three feet high and is a replica of the main idol.

The earlier Utsava Bera which got replaced by Malayappan is called Ugra Srinivasa or Venkataturaivar in Tamil. The idol is about eighteen inches in height and, apart from the Dhruva Bera, may be the oldest idol in Tirumala. This is now the Snapana Bera.[228]

The Bali Bera is called Koluvu Srinivasa. This idol manages the affairs of the temple. The daily calendar is read out to this idol; the day's schedule in the temple is submitted for approval and the daily collections are read out in his presence.[229]

❖

AIR's public broadcast of a classical music programme was the brainchild of Dr B.V. Keskar, the information and broadcasting minister who kicked this off in the early 1950s. He had strong points of view on the educative aspects of public broadcasts and wanted to use these to fulfil the double objectives of moral upliftment and preservation of heritage.[230] Dr Keskar invited all the greatest living exponents of Indian classical music of the time to start broadcasting through AIR. Listeners were treated to a ninety-minute recording to start with, and the best and brightest among the musical fraternity participated. While some found the AIR format restrictive, the resultant recordings constitute one of the greatest archives of classical music anywhere in the world. A scan of these archives throws up unexpected treasures.

One of these is a recording that AIR did in May 1958 of a recitation of the Suprabhātam at the Tirumala temple by a group led by P.V. Ananthasayanam himself. Clearly, his earlier LP was making an impact. Thus, before they settled on M.S. Subbulakshmi, the folks at AIR experimented with other recitations of the Venkateśa Suprabhātam. However, given the stated objective of elevating and entertaining the listening public, AIR decided that a prayer in praise of the most popular deity in India could only be sung by the most popular classical artist of the time.

M.S. Subbulakshmi's recitation made this the best-loved prayer in India and as a by-product, her recording of the Venkateśa Suprabhātam has become the largest selling non-film recording in Indian recording history.

M.S. Subbulakshmi broke prevailing conventions in recording the Venkateśa Suprabhātam for mass broadcast. Devotional prayers are meant for quiet, semi-private rituals and are supposed to be recited by a select few. By fusing her own spiritual journey and her rigorous approach in the recitation, she was able to achieve aesthetic appeal without losing spiritual content. A recent biography states: 'Her renderings were in the traditional mode, more recitational than musical. Yet, she turned her recitation into an aesthetic experience, thanks to her flawless Sanskrit pronunciation. People found that the packaged convenience did not detract any of its sanctity from the recitation … MS single-handedly transformed the culture of morning prayers across south India. She became a member of every worshipping family every morning. This remarkable accomplishment was as a tribute as much to her devotion as to her musical ability.' [231] Her diction is such that her recordings of various prayers are used even now as teaching material where teachers are not available.

The Venkateśa Suprabhātam first became part of the early morning discipline of many households in south India when the daily radio broadcast of the prayer started in the late 1950s as a part of AIR's morning programme. In a terse statement in December 1958, AIR announced that for the Vaikunta Ekadesi festival which fell on the twenty-first of that month, the Sri Venkateśa Suprabhātam would be broadcast from 7.30 a.m. on Madras A and B and Tiruchi wavelengths of AIR Madras. The announcement mentioned that MS would 'render selections from the prayers which are sung at the shrine of Lord Venkateswara at Tirupati every morning, symbolic of awakening the Lord'.[232] Since AIR felt the need to educate the listening public, this may well have been the first public broadcast of the prayer.

The motivating force behind MS's recitational foray was her husband, T. Sadasivam. Founder of the *Kalki* magazine, along with the eponymous Kalki Krishnamurty, Sadasivam was media-savvy and ensured that the magazine had the highest circulation among all weekly magazines. The husband-wife duo, who were intensely religious, were initially hesitant about recording since the concept of women publicly singing religious prayers flew in the face of orthodoxy. It seems they went to the Kanchi paramacharya, Chandrashekarendra Saraswati Swamigal for guidance. The saint of Kanchi gave her the green signal and MS agreed to recite the prayers. Sadasivam thought that a simple temple prayer like the Venkateśa Suprabhātam, if recited by MS, would attain mass popularity and would educate common listeners towards the devotional aspect—bhakti bhava—of Carnatic music. This bit of recursive reasoning seems to have worked beyond all expectations.[233]

२४

mīnākṛte kamaṭhakolanṛsiṃhavarṇin
svāmin paraśvadhatapodhana rāmacandra |
śeṣāṃśarāma yadunandana kalkirūpa
śrīveṅkaṭācalapate tava suprabhātam ||

O one with the form of a fish,
O you who has been a tortoise, boar and a man-lion, O Swamy (Vamana), O you whose penance has been achieved through the use of an axe,
O Ramachandra, O part of Sesha (Balarama),
O joy of the Yadu clan (Krishna), O Kalki,
O Lord of Venkata Hill, arise and protect us.

The famous Dashavataras (ten incarnations of Vishnu) are described in this stanza by Anna and these are a subset of the Vibhava avatara (visible manifestations). This is the concept in the worship of Vishnu that most are familiar with even though they may not have heard of Ramanujacharya or the Azhvaars.

The Vibhava avataras manifest themselves at times when evil becomes particularly ascendant in the world. Most people nowadays have heard of Lord Rama or Lord Krishna. These two are just two of the many Vibhava avataras of Vishnu; there are many more visible manifestations—god has had his hands full with helping creation through the ages.

The enumeration of incarnations in the *Bhagavata Purana* is the best known. The first avataras are the Kumaras who are the brainchildren of Brahma and are manifested in the form of four children. They are also supposed to be tremendously enlightened and realised teachers.

The second avatara is Varaha, the boar who rescued the earth from Rasatala, one of the seven nether worlds. The third avatara is that of the divine sage Narada (he keeps entering the narrative about Vishnu). Since he is also another son of Brahma, incarnations one and three seem to be siblings. There are other instances of sibling reincarnations.

Number four are the divine ascetics, Nara-Narayana. Some versions count these as two separate incarnations.

Incarnation number five is the sage Kapila who disseminated the Sankhya system of philosophy to mankind. The sixth avatara is the sage Dattatreya, son of Anusuya, who was the teacher of Prahlad, among others.

The seventh avatara is Yagya, the son of sage Ruchi and the maiden Akuti who ruled over the Swayambhu Manavantara. The eighth avatara is Rishabhnatha, son of Meru Devi and Nabhi Rai, the first Jain Tirthankar. He is referred to as Urukrama, which means one who has taken great strides.

The ninth avatara is King Prithu, who is supposed to be the first king ever. The tenth is the Matsya avatara which, at the end of one age, guided a ship with all the sages and learned ones till the dawn of the current age. Number eleven is the Kurma or the tortoise which held up the Mandara mountain when gods and demons were using it as the churning stick to churn the ocean. The twelfth incarnation is Dhanavantri, the divine physician, and the thirteenth is Mohini, who beguiles the demons into giving up the nectar to the devas.

The fourteenth incarnation, as Narasimha, tore the powerful lord of the demons with his fingernails after placing him on his thighs. The fifteenth was the one who in three steps covered the three divisions of the universe—the Vamana avatara.

The sixteenth avatara, Parasurama, on seeing kings injure his creator (father), rid the earth of Kshatriyas twenty one times. As we have encountered earlier, Parasurama did this because his mother beat her chest twenty-one times on the death of his father. The seventeenth avatara was born to Satyavati from Parasara and helped ignorant mankind by organising the Vedas into different branches—better known to all as Veda Vyasa.

The eighteenth avatar, as Ramachandra, took the form of the lord of men and, desirous of doing deeds worthy of gods, subjugated even the ocean to attain his ends—i.e., when he crossed over to Lanka. The nineteenth and the twentieth avataras were born among the Vrishni clan as Balarama and Krishna. The twenty-first avatara is a Buddha born in the Kaliyuga to bring back the deluded enemies of gods to the correct path.

The twenty-second avatara will be born in the twilight of the age as a great king named Kali. His coming will mark the end of the world as we know it.[234] Nature will recoil from the current level of wickedness and wipe the slate clean by getting rid of mankind.

The complete list of all Vibhava avataras has thirty-nine separate avataras.[235]

❖

The Venkateśa Suprabhātam had also moved out of south India by then and had reached homes in other parts. An acquaintance of mine remembered hearing it as a boy in Maharashtra in the early 1960s. Apparently, the Bombay A and B stations had started broadcasting the prayer as a starter to a programme of Marathi bhajans. He remembers it very clearly to this day and was able to recall the tune when we met. He said that even though he was not allowed to play the radio at home, his neighbours would play it loudly enough for it to be an unforgettable part of his growing up years. The impact seems to have lingered. A pilgrim I met in Tirumala told me that 30 per cent of the devotees were from Maharashtra. The opportunity for a gramophone recording of MS's recitation would have been self-evident.

MS practised long and hard for the recording of the recitation. In this, as in many others, her daughter, Radha Viswanthan was an integral part of the drill. It is from Mrs Viswanathan's account to her son that we know that the practice lasted for a couple of hours a day for many months—from the first few months of her pregnancy to a few days before her second child, V. Shrinivasan, was born.

MS insisted on perfection and the duo's diction in this recitation and in others was buttressed by practice with various traditional scholars. P.V. Ananthasyanam Iyengar himself was deputed by the TTD to train her in the recitation of the Suprabhātam. The great scholar, Agnihotram Tatacharyar was present in some of the later training sessions and made corrections as he saw fit. Another scholar, Dr Veezhinathan, has, in recent TV clips, also mentioned how MS would seek feedback and would unhesitatingly agree to recite again if even the slightest error was pointed out.

Left to herself, MS might have continued honing her recitation, but Radha Viswanathan insisted that the recording be done before her impending delivery. Dry runs were done and even a live recitation in Tirumala in front of Lord Venkateswara was conducted. The recording at the HMV studio was done in front of a garlanded portrait of Lord Venkateswara. The hard work paid off. The duo's recitation of the Venkateśa Suprabhātam was perfect and the recording was done in two takes. It seems the first recording itself was flawless, but a second was taken to be on the safe side. The recording engineer, S.K. Sen, was brought down from Calcutta. More than five decades later, Sen is still fondly remembered for his skill and disposition by his successor, K.S. 'HMV Raghu' Raghunathan.

V. Shrinivasan was born within a week of the recording. Mrs Viswanathan determined that since she had spent most of the term reciting the Venkateśa Suprabhātam, if the child was a boy, he would be called Shrinivasan, and if a girl, she would be called Padmavati. The first royalty received by MS from the recording was given to the Kanchi Kamakoti Peetham, but the Paramacharya requested the Sadasivams to donate all royalties to Tirupati since it rightfully belonged to Lord Venkateswara.[236]

The gramophone recording of the Suprabhātam was first released for sale by President S. Radhakrishnan during the Tenth Radio Sangeet Sammelan of the All India Radio in November 1963. The idealistic glow of the first decade of independence had got a check of realpolitik as people coped with the trauma of an earlier Chinese aggression. Everywhere, people were seeking solace in the familiar. The president's speech at the launch gives an insight into the nation's mood and sets the context for why the prayer was considered important in those times. In his address, the president initially struck a sombre note and referred to the difficult times of the previous months. He hoped that pieces of devotional music such as the Venkateśa Suprabhātam would keep reminding people about the core values underlying the nation's traditions and help them find solace in difficult times. He rounded off by saying 'the play goes on, though the actors may change. If we are great inheritors of traditions of the country, we should stand up for the right and defend against the assaults by wrong'. He ended his speech by praising MS.[237] While the president was echoing basic truths, lesser folk would have listened to the prayer more as a daily discipline and for the sense of joy that it conveyed.

By the late 1960s, MS's recitation had started to impact listeners in unimagined ways. Sripati Sridhar, an artist from Rajahmundry, decided to do a painting for each of the verses of the Venkateśa Suprabhātam and the three accompanying prayers. He took a vow of silence and started painting in 1967. He completed his works by 1973 and was still observing the vow even as late as 1975.[238] This painting collection became a travelling exhibition that went to many parts of the peninsula. Eventually, the TTD purchased the entire set for Rs 17,000 and put it up for display.

२५

elālavaṅgaghanasārasugandhitīrthaṃ
divyaṃ viyatsariti hemaghaṭeṣu pūrṇam |
dhṛtavādyavaidikaśikhāmaṇayaḥ prahṛṣṭāḥ tiṣṭhanti
veṅkaṭapate tava suprabhātam ||

Priests who are well versed in the Vedas and other scriptures are eagerly awaiting your audience bearing golden pots of water from the Ganga which falls from the sky and is scented with cloves, cardamom and camphor.

Akash Ganga Pond is also called Viyatsarita in some sources. The traditional story of the Akash Ganga Pond is a miraculous one. Tirumala Nambi, the maternal uncle of Ramanujacharya (tenth century CE) had made a daily practice of filling a pot from a lake called Papavinaasha

Tirtham and taking the same to hand it over to the archakas at the temple in Tirumala. This would have been a long, hard walk, as even today the trip to the Papavinasham (which is now a reservoir with a dam) involves a twenty-minute jeep ride into a reserved forest. One day, as he filled his pot and started the trek back to the temple, Lord Venkateswara appeared before him in the form of a hunter and asked him for some water to quench his thirst. Tirumalai Nambi refused saying it was meant for the rituals at the temple, and he continued on his way. But the hunter would not give up. As Nambi walked lost in his musings, the hunter pierced the pot with an arrow and drank his fill. After a while, Tirumala Nambi realised what had happened and raged at the hunter. But the hunter in turn said, 'Grandfather, you do not have to go back to the Papavinasha Tirtham all the way. I will show you a beautiful source of clean water.' He took him down the valley to a secluded spot. There was no source of water there. But before Nambi could start scolding him again, the hunter shot an arrow towards the top of a mountain, from where water came out in gushes. After revealing his true form, Lord Venkateswara vanished. Tirumala Nambi was overwhelmed with joy that the lord had played a prank on him and addressed him as Grandfather. He was able to reach the temple in time with the water from the newly-created waterbody. The newly created waterbody is called the Akash Ganga Tirtha, and even today water can be seen seeping through the rocks.

As recounted earlier, Anna was tasked with the responsibility of getting the water and scenting it a few centuries later. By his time, the water pots must have been made with much costlier materials. Hence the description 'hemaghatesu' or 'in golden pots'.

The tradition is that, through the night, Brahma worships Lord Venkateswara, and five cups of water which have been scented with spices are left every night for him to fulfill the prescribed rituals.

The worship that the priests offer to Lord Venkateswara is therefore the second level of prayers that are offered on behalf of the general public. The first worship of the day which is conducted by humans is the Visvarupaseva, better known as the Suprabhata Seva.

The Suprabhata Seva itself is conducted behind a screen in the sanctum sanctorum. It has been described in detail by Dr M.S. Ramesh in her work on the festivals and rituals of the temple and the following description draws on her account.[239]

Early in the morning, a cowherd goes to the residences of the priests scheduled to conduct the ceremony for that day and wakes them. The priest follows the cowherd, who carries a firebrand, with a set of keys to the sanctum in his hand. The cowherd then fetches the jiyyangar, who carries a second set of keys. The representative of the temple's management then arrives with the third set of keys. This triplicate system is used for the 'Bangaru Vakkili'—Telugu for the 'golden doorway'. Once this is opened, the officiating priests go in and the door is closed from within.

By this time, the devotees who wish to witness the Suprabhata Seva assemble. The recitation of the Suprabhātam and the three other prayers—Stotra, Prapatti, and Mangalasasana begins.

Inside the sanctum, all the lamps are lit. The Bhoga Srinivasa idol, which has been recumbent since the

Ekanta Seva of the previous evening, is ceremonially awakened. This idol is then taken to a spot near the left foot of the main idol, the Dhruva Bera. The small idol is symbolically connected to the main idol with a bunch of thirty-two blades of Darbha-grass which are knotted. The front portion is said to represent Brahma, the knot Vishnu, and the rest, Rudra.[240] The cot and other accessories from the previous night's Ekanta Seva are cleared. By the time the final strains of the last verse are being heard outside the sanctum, the aarthi is being done inside for the main idol.

The devotees are allowed to come closer and they surge towards the point called 'Kulasekharpaddi', or 'Kulasekhar's step', for a closer look. This is the only time during the day that the devotees get to see Lord Venkateswara's feet.

After the Suprabhata Seva is over, the ritual cleaning takes place and the preparations are made for the next sequence of prayers and rituals.[241]

❖

My mother has vivid memories of the Suprabhata Seva at Tirumala in the 1970s. She first visited the temple as a young girl in the early 1950s, but her regular visits started from the late 1960s.

In her own words: 'Every year, it was a part of my schedule to visit Tirumala on my visit to Chennai from Delhi. In the early years, we were able to have darshan without waiting, without payments and any number of times without any difficulty.'

She first attended the Suprabhata Seva in 1971. She used to do a type of worship called the Anga

Pradakshina, and till the mid-80s at least, those who did an Anga Pradakshina around the main sanctum were automatically allowed to stand near those who recited the Venkateśa Suprabhātam. From 1971 till about 1990, my parents visited Tirumala every year. Trips to Tirumala were an annual feature of our vacation away from Delhi. My mother did a pradakshina almost every year as well. Hence my abiding memory of visits to Tirumala as a child were of my mother leaving the guest house before 2.30 a.m. for a bath in the Swami Pushkarni so that she could be among the first in the queue for the Anga Pradakshina. My father would dutifully follow. They would get an automatic entry to the recitation of the Venkateśa Suprabhātam without any restraints. Inside the sanctum sanctorum, there would be no pushing or jostling as very few people would come for this service in those years.

My mother remembers that there were no restrictions for devotees. Once the devotees were assembled inside, the priests who were to recite on that day would take their positions in two rows facing each other. Each row would have six priests. Only two senior priests would have the mikes placed before them. The recitation would begin in one voice and would flow flawlessly. The moment the recitation was over, the officiating priest would go into the sanctum and have the first seva of Lord Venkateswara.

In 1984, my parents, who were justifiably downbeat about my prospects in the Class Ten Boards, had made a vow to Lord Venkateswara, that immediately after my ICSE exam, I would do an Anga Pradakshina. So, after the boards, it was straight to Tirumala. After the first three rotations, the pradakshina seemed to happen by itself and I was among the early finishers. I was ushered into the sanctum, slightly giddy, just in time to hear the chorus start the recitation of the Venkateśa Suprabhātam.

In those years, there was no charge for attending the Suprabhata Seva. After the recitation, the door of the sanctum would be opened; all would go inside to seek blessings. The number of people at the recital would be around 200 as not too many would brave the nippy early hours on the hilltop. Through the year, my mother would wait for this visit. I have always wondered at this seemingly strange level of devotion, but I guess it kept them cheerful through the terrible decade of the 1980s in Delhi, which included my younger brother's near-fatal illness, and the sickness and closure of the company in which my father was working.

As years went by, attending the Suprabhata Seva became tougher for my folks. Age precluded the physical rigour of the Anga Pradakshina. The Seva itself became paid and my folks would reach a day earlier and line up to buy tickets for the next morning. Initially, the tickets were reasonably priced and easily available. Later on, getting tickets became tougher and they had to be bought from a bank. My folks still went.

As more and more devotees started thronging the temple, many new rules and regulations came into force and things reached a stage when the waiting list for tickets was a few months long. My folks decided that after so many continuous years of easy darshan of Lord Venkateswara perhaps it was best if others should now get the chance. They stopped their annual trip to

Tirumala. Now they take the occasional package tour to Tirumala offered by KSRTDC which leaves Bengaluru in the morning and returns late the next day after a complete round of the holy places.

२६

bhāsvānudeti vikacāni saroruhāṇi
sampūrayanti ninadaiḥ kakubho vihaṅgāḥ |
śrīvaiṣṇavāḥ satatamarthitamaṅgalāste
dhāmāśrayanti tava veṅkaṭa suprabhātam ||

The sun is now overhead and the half-open lilies have blossomed completely. The birds make all the directions echo with their songs. Your devotees who constantly seek liberation for the entire universe surrender themselves to your protection for salvation.

❖

As the 1970s gave way to the 1980s, amidst other changes, India also saw a boom in consumer electronics. Colour TV made headlines but the two-in-one cassette player played an equal role in determining popular culture. New recording labels mushroomed and film music became even more popular. Notwithstanding this, MS's recording of the Venkateśa Suprabhātam became even more pervasive as cassettes of the prayer became bestsellers. Much before that, electronic dealers in India started giving away a free cassette of the Suprabhātam with the purchase of every 'two-in-one'—apparently many customers wished to 'inaugurate' the new appliance by listening to the prayer. It could now be heard everywhere—tea shops and trucks included.

By the 1990s, this recitation had become a part of the popular culture of south India—it had traversed a long distance from the quiet, semi-private recitation of a few decades earlier, and an even greater distance from what may have been an irregular recitation by a handful at the end of the seventeenth century. In 1999, the Adyar Library and Research Centre (ALRC) released an edition of the Venkateśa Suprabhātam with a translation and a very brief exposition of some of the verses. This was done by Professor T. Venkatacharya, a famous Sanskrit scholar who taught at the University of Toronto. While the ALRC itself has many manuscripts of Suprabhātams to various deities and some interesting versions of the Venkateśa Suprabhātam itself, Professor Venkatacharya preferred to base his work on the version released by the TTD. The Professor's exegesis is authoritative and at the same time, expressed in simple language.

While it does not say so anywhere in the foreword or the introduction, the ALRC's publication mirrored the popularity that the hymn's recitation by M.S. Subbulakshmi enjoyed. By this time, MS herself seems to have become completely detached from things like fame and wealth. Her worldview at the time is best summed up by a press release by T. Sadashivam, her husband in 1990: 'There has been news in the press recently that M.S. Subbulakshmi donated about Rs. 20 lakh to the Tirurnala Tirupathi Devasthanams. The news is not entirely correct. The fact is M.S. Subbulakshmi renounced her royalty in favour of the TTD when she rendered Sri Venkateswara Suprabatham. The royalties accrued from the sale of these ... have gone to TTD periodically which really means that ... the amount has been donated to the Lord of the Seven Hills by the many devotees of the Lord who purchased the records ... Subbulakshmi has been just an instrument in this sublime cause.'[242]

२७

Brahmādayassuravarāssamaharṣayaste
santassanandanmukhstvatha yogivaryāḥ |
dhāmāntike tava hi maṅgalavastuhastāḥ
śrīveṅkaṭācalapate tava suprabhātam ||

All the gods led by Brahma, the sages and the saints led by Sanandana wait outside the door for your summons, with auspicious items in their hands. Good morning, O Lord of Venkatachala.

The recitation of Tirupalli Ezhuchchi of Tonda Adi Podi Azhvaar provided the impetus for the composition of the Venkateśa Suprabhātam. The parallels cannot be escaped and it is interesting to look at both the prayers side by side.[243]

The Tirupalli Ezhuchchi is only ten verses and hence may seem like a subset of the Venkateśa Suprabhātam but, actually, the Venkateśa Suprabhātam is an elaboration of the themes that are presented in this prayer.

The superficial difference between the poems is that one is addressed to Lord Ranganatha in Srirangam and the other to Lord Venkateswara in Tirumala. Ezhuchchi draws heavily on the Ramayana in the address to god, while, apart from the first verse, the Venkateśa Suprabhātam only mentions the Rama avatara as one among the many manifestations. It starts the first verse with Rama being asked to get up to do all his daily duties while the Tirupalli Ezhuchchi echoes this later in its fourth verse with a specific mention of his job of protecting the hermitages of the sages during sacrifices. Sounds of the sea and of water abound in the Ezhuchchi, perhaps because Srirangam is an island on the Kaveri, while the Suprabhātam has a verse on the sacred waterbody near the temple. The Ezhuchchi is silent on Lakshmi, while the Suprabhātam has two verses right at the beginning propitiating the goddess.

The similarities are deeper and stronger. Anna would have known the Ezhuchchi intimately and perhaps would have recited it many times himself.

The obvious common factor is the evocative description of nature in both the prayers. Bees, birds, stars, and wafting fragrances all combine to create a similar mood in both of them. The other common feature is the description of the many types of celestial and non-celestial beings who gather for prayer.

The first verse of the Ezhuchchi talks about the sunrise in the east, the assemblage of gods and the blossoming of flowers. The second verse of the Ezhuchchi talks about gently wafting breezes that carry the fragrances of flowers in the forest—the term used is 'mullai', which is the categorisation of forests in Sangam literature. The flower 'mullai' is a type of jasmine. The third verse starts with the spread of dawn and the disappearance of stars. The Ezhuchchi talks about areca fronds blooming, as does the Suprabhātam—so, obviously, this is an important sign of mornings in south peninsular India.

The Ezhuchchi then introduces sounds from the cattle sheds—sounds of cattle and of cowherds and bees and bumble bees make their appearance. The repetition of such themes points to an intimate association with the markers of daily life.

The Ezhuchchi has birds chirping in groves while, the Suprabhātam has them chirping in cages in the eighth verse and calling cacophonously in forest valleys in the seventeenth. In the Ezhuchchi, gods and priests gather with garlands and scented water, which they also do close to the end of the Suprabhātam. The sun god, six-faced Subrahmanya (Kartikeya), the Rudras, Adityas, Maruts, Vasus, and the entire celestial cast are all mentioned by the Tirupalli Ezhuchchi. Crowding by devotees who jostle (like they do now) is described in both of them. The action in the Ezhuchchi is far more urgent and the imagery repeatedly depicts the press of bodies of celestial beings, gods, sages, humans, etc., jostling to worship Lord Ranganatha—relatable to those who have been in the rough and tumble of modern-day south Indian temple visits. To that extent, the mood in the Venkateśa Suprabhātam is a lot more relaxed and the description is strung out over a lot more verses. However, nowadays, the jostling at Tirumala is far more intense than what is experienced at Srirangam.

Indra is mentioned again and very prominently in the Tirupalli Ezhuchchi as opposed to his being part of the throng of gods in the Suprabhātam. Perhaps he was still one of the most prominent in the pantheon in those times and the passing mention in the fourteenth century prayer is an indicator of the decline in his importance.

In the Tirupalli Ezhuchchi, Narada appears along with the sage Tamburu who is now almost unknown in popular culture. Suprabhātam has a whole verse to Narada, but no Tamburu. The ninth verse of the Ezhuchchi talks about the music of stringed instruments, praise by all celestials, etc., and the Suprabhātam mentions these in different verses.

By verse ten in the Ezhuchchi, the lotuses have fully blossomed, or in other words, the sun has come up. The verse talks about ladies who have bathed and are probably queuing up for a glimpse. It signs off with the benediction that the tulsi garland of the poet (by which the Azhvaar probably also means the poem) be accepted.

A deeper common theme between both the poems, of course, is in the premise that the god is not actually asleep but is in a state of deep inner reflection. Both the poems are an exhortation and request to the god to move his gaze outwards in order to oversee and hence protect the world. Imagine the god as the deep meditator who is happiest in internal contemplation. Every morning, this god is importuned by a jostling and noisy group of immortals and mortals to start looking after them and the general well-being of the world.

In the deepest sense, both prayers are appeals and carry the message of surrender of the self to the higher power. It is also central to many other routes to liberation that are extant in the country. While conceptually this business of surrender is easy to understand, the sublime faith required for that is easier to preach than to practise.

❖

M.S. Subbulakshmi passed away in 2004. The outpouring of grief was widespread and spontaneous. The impact that her rendition of the Venkateśa Suprabhātam had on popular consciousness was best captured by veteran journalist A.J. Phillip, who recalled his childhood memories in his obituary message to her:

We lived at the foot of Chuttipara, a mountainous rock that spread over a square kilometre. Legend has it that Ram and Sita spent some time in a cave on this rock during their 'vanvas'. A bed-like piece of rock in the cave is believed to have served as the bed for the Prince of Ayodhya.

On holidays, we children used to climb up the rock from where we had a panoramic view of Pathanamthitta town. We never dared to enter the cave for fear of the unknown.

One morning, we woke up to hear that an idol of a god was found on the rock. The news spread like wildfire and people in thousands from far and near began flocking to the makeshift temple that was soon erected on the rock.

The shrine acquired a powerful mike set donated by a rich devotee. It would come alive on the dot at 5 a.m. with a recorded Carnatic rendition. We would wake up with a jerk as one of the loudspeakers was directly pointed at us. My mother was the first to see an opportunity in the unsolicited alarm service of the temple. Why not ask us to get up and study?

So it became a regular feature for us to get up at five hearing the devotional song …

Mother could only force us to open the books and not persuade us to read them. Often, I pretended to be reading the books. Gradually, the inevitable happened. I began listening to the stotras that wafted through the air. The Sanskrit verses were all Greek to me. Yet, I began liking the mesmeric voice.

It was Sri Venkateswara Suprabhātam sung by M.S. Subbulakshmi. Unconsciously, my tryst with Carnatic music had begun.

> It did not take long for me to become a fan of MS as she was widely known. My mornings were never complete if I did not hear her Suprabhātam.
>
> The routine continued for several years and I never found the stotras to Sri Venkateswara repetitive or a bore. With each listening, I felt that its appeal grew greater and greater for me. In fact, her renderings brought the realisation that language, religion and caste were no bar to enjoy good songs sung with sincerity and devotion.
>
> MS broke the stereotype that the North Indians did not like Carnatic music as her concerts, whether at Patiala or in Patna, were always a hit. Little did I realise then that she had also proved to the contrary that Christians did not like Hindu devotional songs.[244]

Mrs Radha Viswanathan started performing once again in 2007, after a gap of fifteen years, along with her granddaughter S. Aishwarya. In 2010, forty-seven years after the original recording, she and her granddaughter did a video recording of the Venkateśa Suprabhātam for the Shankar Mahadevan Academy. This was done as a teaching aid for future generations of learners—apparently, even after five decades, her intonation, memory, and diction were perfect.

Radha's final performance in Tirumala was along with her granddaughter S Aishwarya on 16 September 2010 (the ninety-fourth birth anniversary of MS). The TTD had made special arrangements for Radha and her party to get a close darshan of the lord even though she was in a wheelchair. Radha and Aishwarya sang in front of the lord uninterrupted for forty-five minutes.

By the first decade of the twenty-first century, M.S. Subbulakshmi's recording of the Venkateśa Suprabhātam had become one of the largest selling records of all time in Indian recording history. A recent newspaper article underlines the durability of the recording. Quoting S. Sankaranarayanan, retired Marketing Manager, HMV (now Saregama), the article says: 'Whenever the turnover decreased, it became a regular practice to issue … copies of the Suprabhātam … No distributor or retailer ever refused, or returned copies unsold.'[245]

२८

lakṣmīnivāsa niravadyaguṇaikasindho
saṃsārasāgarasamuttaraṇaikaseto |
vedāntavedya nijavaibhavabhaktabhogya
śrīveṅkaṭācalapate tava suprabhātam ||

O abode of Lakshmi, O sole ocean of all virtues, O essence of all the Vedantas, One who is both known through the Vedantas and whose realisation leads to the knowledge of the Vedantas—therefore One who is both the cause and the effect of all self-realisation, O one who ameliorates the burdens of an earthly existence and liberates from the cycle of rebirths, O faultless one, O Lord of the Venkata Hill, Good Morning to you.

The last type of manifestation of Vishnu is the Antaryami avatara—the manifestation of God within each living being.

This manifestation of Vishnu is present within each one of us. It is up to each of us to train our consciousness in order to try to perceive it. The Antaryami form needs you to lead a moderate life, be mindful, and be grateful for small, everyday occurrences. Through this method, you become quieter within and hence start experiencing the Godhead inside yourself.

Inanimate beings can also be an avatara—which is an incarnation. The message that there is the divine in nature is consistent.

❖

In Tirumala, the Suprabhata Seva became one of the most sought-after prayer rituals and the Seva's attractiveness meant that the authorities had to contend with larger and larger crowds.

Currently, the demand for attendance in the Suprabhata Seva and the other special services is so much that the TTD has instituted a digital lottery to determine who may attend. From the fifth to the seventh or the eighth of every month, those who want to attend the Suprabhata Seva are requested to register online for a date three months in advance. A day or two later, at midnight, an electronic 'dip' picks a select number of devotees who are then asked to pay the token fee for entry to the service.[246] I tried the dip a few times in 2019 but remained unlucky and hence have not attended the modern version of the Suprabhata Seva.

Other ways of visiting the temple that are more certain, are either through booking a slot by buying a token or just lining up in the queue complexes that are built to house pilgrims. Joining the queue complex can involve waiting periods of up to twenty hours before the pilgrim is admitted into the sanctum sanctorum. While all creature comforts are taken care of, the time taken will test the depth of the pilgrim's devotion. If one is uninclined or unable to pay the various 'Special Entry' tokens, a strenuous method of jumping the line is to walk up the hill as was the practice before the motorable road was laid. Those who walk up are allowed entry into a service called 'Divya Darshan', which involves around three to five hours of waiting.

Walking up is also a good way to try experiencing the natural beauty that Anna repeatedly evokes in the prayer. As mentioned earlier, the poem, Sri Venkateśa Seva Krama, was composed as a description of a pilgrim's journey from the bottom of the hill to the doorstep of Lord Venkateswara.

There are two popular routes to walk up the holy hill—one from Alipiri near the Tirumala bypass on the road up the Hill, and another steeper route through Srivari Mettu which is from the Chandragiri side. There are some other routes but they are now rarely used and the restrictions that are in place to combat the poaching of the Red Sanders tree has made many areas of the Seshachala out-of-bounds. This is a pity, as those who have walked atop the holy hill and have visited the forests of Seshachala, before the restrictions came into force, talk about its breathtaking natural beauty.

The Alipiri route opens at 4 a.m. and many pilgrims like an early start. In earlier times, this pathway was very difficult and pilgrims faced many difficulties and dangers while walking up. An important initiative that the TTD took was to make this walk a pleasant and easy experience for all devotees. The comfort of the pilgrims became the paramount consideration while renovating the path.[247] The old hill path has given way to a covered concrete walkway. Due to the awning over the walkway, it is difficult to follow the imagery of the poets—the vistas that inspired them are no longer visible. There are tea stalls at every fifty yards or so, serving snacks and beverages. Since the climb is now easy for most, the really devout, who like the rigour, do things differently from the rest. I saw a couple of youths walking up part of the way on their knees, and one lady was daubing each of the three thousand plus steps leading to the top with vermilion.

The first thousand steps are steeper and involve some effort. Once one reaches Gali Gopuram, there is respite on the gradient. A long row of eateries offers more relief. Here, the pilgrims get the entry card which will give them the estimated time of entry into the queue complex.

The composer of the Seva Karma talks about peacocks, koels, parakeets, and mynas and how their calls gladden the soul. Anna talks about how the valleys resound with the calls of birds and beasts greeting the dawn. On the path, these could not be experienced, but small uncovered sections were rewarding—a shy junglefowl skittered into the undergrowth, babblers browsed unconcerned, bulbuls flitted about, a magpie robin unblinkingly stared me down, swifts glided—giving brief glimpses of a bird heaven.

A deer park provides respite and a clearing with a gigantic banyan tree and stone benches is a peaceful digression. There are palmyra and silk cotton trees. The poet mentions the Chandan tree which can also mean the Red Sanders—these forests are under siege from poachers who seek the wood of this tree for the Chinese market.

The path crosses the road at a few points and now there are cleverly constructed tunnels which help with the crossing. Closer to the top, at intervals, the traveller can see the statues of the Azhvaars mentioned earlier.

The path ends suddenly as does the relative peace and one is back in the tumult of the multitudes who are the constant feature of Tirumala.

During my visit, the walkers were allowed to join the queue at the appointed time. The queue was onerous but, remarkably, most of the folk remained patient and good-humoured. The wait may have been longer than usual and, initially, there was fretting and anger as people talked about missed trains and disrupted schedules. After a while, everyone seemed to let go and become content in allowing things to happen as they would. After a six-hour vigil which tested the sense of surrender to the utmost, my batch was liberated from the queue complex and joined the throng of devotees. I was lucky—many had waited for twenty hours or more. The line snaked along the wall, and looking out one realised that the landmarks of childhood visits no longer exist. Only the shrine to Tirumalai Nambi is recognisable. The earlier stone slabs, worn by centuries of pilgrims, were much cooler and pleasant to walk on compared to the concrete paving.

Of the main four temples to Vishnu in south India, the Tirumala temple leaves one with the least sense of space. Srirangam is a town by itself and one can lose oneself inside the temple. The Varadaraja Perumal Temple in Kanchipuram is vast and all of Melkote town melds into the Yadavachalapati Temple. It may be due to the fact that large parts of the temple are no longer accessible to common folk or the fact that other temples do not get these many devotees.

The Bangaru Vakili seems even smaller and individual identity is lost as the crowd takes a life of its own. There is a surge towards the sanctum and one is carried there without effort. In front of the sanctum itself, the multitude no longer matters.

Afterwards, everyone seems quieter and happier. After visiting the sanctum, the frenzied crowds become amazingly peaceful—it's a remarkable transformation. Small things make folk laugh. People lining up to collect the famous laddu are no longer irritable—a lady who uses her small child to jump the queue for the prasadam is admired for her 'technical game' in rustic Telugu—and fellow-feeling is on full display.

One is also struck by the extraordinary complexity of keeping the temple running while hosting such a crowd of devotees, many of whom are almost berserk with devotional fervour. The TTD hires a special breed of people who serve without any expectation of gratitude—the one person I thanked seemed shocked at the compliment.

It is late at night and there is a pleasant chill in the air by the time one leaves the temple complex. The return journey is unexpectedly smooth in every way. Buses seem to materialise by themselves and the conductors indulgently stop wherever passengers want. The last trains have left, but deluxe buses ply through the night. They cover distances faster, and the weary but peaceful traveller reaches home earlier than planned.

२९

itthaṃ vṛṣācalapaterihasuprabhātaṃ
ye mānavāḥ pratidinaṃ paṭhituṃ pravṛttāḥ |
teṣāṃ prabhātasamaye smṛtiraṅgabhājāṃ
prajñāṃ parārthasulabhāṃ paramāṃ prasūte ||

Human beings who greet you, the Lord of Vrisha Hill, in this fashion every day in the morning by reciting this morning prayer, attain that state of highest realisation, which is the essence of all the teachings of the liberated sages and which is beyond all description.

The implication here is that even good intention is enough. How the listener relates to the prayer is entirely up to him. At its easiest, it can be related to as a daily appeal to a friendly higher power. At a deeper level, it is an attempt at self-purification through self-realisation. As with every other aspect of the system, there is no dogma here and that makes this prayer so universal.

Since times immemorial, the temple of Lord Venkateswara in Tirumala has allowed devotees to visit every day and no one remembers the temple ever having shut. However, due to COVID-19, the temple was closed to devotees in the early part of 2020.[248] When the Venkateśa Suprabhātam would have been recited during the lock down, it would have been a private recitation attended by a handful of temple attendants. The wheel has, thus, come full circle after three hundred years—a handful of temple servants made their way through the forests amidst invasions and chaos to offer service to Lord Venkateswara in earlier times, and another handful of dedicated priests and attendants ignore disease and infection to offer prayers now. Sublime faith is the common factor.

Through history, a remarkably diverse group have offered Lord Venkateswara their love and service. Lord Venkateswara seems to find more and more adherents as the years roll on. Such timeless devotion is the result of the universality of his appeal, and the Venkateśa Suprabhātam endures as it reinforces this by its celebration of the divine in day-to-day life.

In these times of uncertainty, this prayer—which celebrates the divine in the mundane and is dedicated to a deity who is the personal go-to agency for all matters for millions—assumes far greater importance than is traditionally accorded to it and will hopefully continue to inspire and elevate its listeners. The pandemic will pass and devotees will throng Tirumala again. As new listeners emerge and as the older listeners find new things to like about the Venkateśa Suprabhātam, it is important that the listeners remember all those—celebrated or obscure—who sustained this prayer as a living tradition through thick and thin for the last six centuries. Doing so makes one remember that faith is born and sustained in humility.

POSTSCRIPT

A lot of work on understanding this prayer still remains to be done as it was outside my capabilities or reach. The other three prayers namely the Sri Venkateśa Stotra, the Sri Venkateśa Prapatti and the Sri Venkateśa Magalasasam complete the entire recitation of the Suprabhātam. They are full of mystical significance and require far deeper learning for any exposition. Their texts and a simple translation in English may be seen in the translations of the Venkateśa Suprabhātam by the TTD or in the exposition in English by Prof. T. Venkatacharya published by the Adyar Library.

Given the overwhelming popularity of all the four prayers, a traditional commentary in print is long overdue. Fortunately for us, a start has been made by Sri K.V. Raghavacharya in Telugu.

More work on the history will be equally rewarding. An exhaustive textual survey of all the extant manuscripts of the Venkateśa Suprabhātam may provide a better sense of the history of the recitation. The records at Tirumala, including the Sawal-e-Jawab Patti, could surely throw up a lot more information on this subject. There is a Marathi manuscript listed in the GOML, Madras called the *Tirumala Devsatana Nitya Karma va*

Puja which was written by a certain Narain Rao Shastri and records the rituals in Tirumala circa 1750 CE when the Marathas briefly administered the temple—whoever publishes it will be doing great service to posterity. The English era records in various repositories are a constant source of new material on all aspects of our country's history and who knows what aspects of this prayer will come to light in the years to come as they are mined.

I hope that someone with greater ability will perhaps walk this path again and will bring greater understanding about this lovely prayer in the future.

SELECT BIBLIOGRAPHY

Primary Sources

Srimad Ramayanam by Maharishi Valmiki, Volume 1, *Balakandam.* Webolim (2012).

Sri Venkateśa Suprabhātam p. 1 in *Sri Venkateśa Kavya Kalapa,* Tirupati: Tirmala Tirupati Devasthanams. (1946).

Sri Venkateswara Suprabhātam (trans. by B.V.L. Narayana Row), Tirupati: Tirmala Tirupati Devasthanams. (1999).

Sri Venkateśa Suprabhata Manajri Varivasya Vyakhya Sahitamau—Telugu commentary by Sri K.V. Raghavacharya. Tirupati: Poreetha Prachaurana Sanstha (2014). Translated from the Telugu to English by Sri Mahadeva Sarma.

Sri Venkateśa Suprabhata. With an exposition in English by T. Venkatacharya, The Adyar Library and Research Centre, Adyar, Chennai (1999).

Sri Venkatachala Mahatmayam. Tirupati: Tirmala Tirupati Devasthanams. (1959–60).

Sri Vishnu Puranam. Kanchipuram: Commemorative volume published as part of the 600 birth celebration of Manavala Mamunigal by P.B. Anagaracharya. Parashara, M. (1972).

Bhagavata Purana. sanskritdocuments.org. (2018).

Parasara Bhatta, *Sri Vishnu Sahasranama Bhashya,* Visishtadvaita Pracharini Sabha trans. by Prof. A. Srinivasa Raghavan, Mylapore, Madras (1959).

Sri Ramanuja Gita Bhashya Madras trans. by Swami Adidevananda, Sri Ramakrishna Math, Mylapore, Madras.

Sangeeta Ratnakara of Sarangadeva—part 2. ed. V.G. Apte, Anandashrama Sanskrit Granthavali, Anandashram Press. (1942).

Brihat Samhita of Varahamihira. *English Translation with Notes by V.S. Sastri and M.R. Bhat.* Bangalore: V.B. Soobiah and Sons (Digitised by H.P. Das) (1946).

Krisnamacharya, P. *Kainkaryaratnavalli.* Tirupati: SVU Oriental Series 26, Oriental Research Institute, Sri Venkateswara University (1993).

Yateendra Pravana Prabhavam, composed by Swamy Pillailokam Jeeyar, edited by Ramanujam V.V. Published in 1992. With financial assistance from Tirumala Tirupati Devasthanams

Prapannamritam by Ananatcharya, Mumbai (1964).

Raghavacharya *Sri Suktam (*Hindi translation*)*, Acharyagranthamala (1961).

Bharati, S. *The Sacred Book of Four Thousand.* Chennai: Sri Rama Bharati. (2000).

Vādibhīkaraguruparamparāślokāḥ, R No. 6350 in Trennial Catalogue of Manuscripts collected from 1937–38 to 1939–40, GOML, Madras (1950).

Secondary Sources

Sridhara Babu, D. (1990). *Hayagriva The Horse-headed Diety in Indian Culture.* Tirupati: Sri Venkateshwara University Oriental Research Institute, Tirupati.

Banerjea, J.N. (1941). *The Development of Hindu Iconography.* Calcutta: University of Calcutta.

Basavaraju, Sridhar V. (2015). *The Priest of Tirumala.* Sridhar V. Basavaraju.

D'Huy, J. (2013). A Cosmic Hunt in the Berber Sky: A Phylogenetic Reconstruction of a Palaeolithic Mythology. *Les Cahiers de l'AARS, Saint-Lizier: Association des amis de l'art rupestre saharien*, pp. 93–106.

Dave, K.N. (2005). *Birds in Sanskrit Literature.* Delhi: Motilal Banarsidass.

Dikshit, S.B. (1969). *History of Indian Astronomy Part 1.* Tr. R.V. Vaidya, Delhi: Manager of Publications, Issued under Authority of Director General, IMD.

E.R.H.S.S. Ediriweera, N.Y.S. Premarathna. 'Medicinal and cosmetic uses of Bee's Honey - A review'. AYU, April-June 2012, Vol. 33, Issue 2, pp. 178-182.

Extracts from the Report of the Hindu Religious Endowments Commission. (1960–62).

George, T.J.S. (2016). *M.S. Subbulakshmi—The Definitive Biography.* New Delhi: Aleph Book Company.

Govindacharya, A. (1906). *The Life of Ramanujacharya.* S Murthy & Co., Madras.

Govindacharya, A. (1902), *The Holy Lives of Azhvars or The Dravida Saints*. Mysore: GTA Press.

Husain, M. (1976). *The Rehla of Ibn Battuta.* Baroda: Oriental Institute, The Maharaja Sayaji Rao University.

Irvine, N.M. (1907). *Storia do Mogor or Mogul India 1653–1708 Vol III.* London: John Murray. Albemarle Street.

Iyengar, S.K. (1939). *A History of the Holy Shrine of Sri Venkateśa in Tirupati (Two volumes).* Madras: Printed at Ananda Press.

Jagadeesan, N. (1989). *Collected papers on Tamil Vaishnavism.* Madurai: With financial assistance from TTD.

Jagannathan, S. (1994). *Impact of Sri Ramanujacharya on Temple Worship.* Delhi: Nag Publishers.

Jayaraj, J.S. (n.d.). *Early Hunter-Gatherers Adaptations in the Tirupati Valley.* Tirupati: S.V. University, Tirupati.

Prasad P.V.K. (2017). *When I saw Tirupati Balaji.* Hyderabad: EMESCO Books.

Karttunen, K. (2015). 'Bhramarotpītādharaḥ: Bees in Classical India'. *Studia Orientalia Electronica, 107,* 89–134.

Subrahmanya Kumar, V.V. (1989). *Sacred Shrines of Tirupati.* Tirupati: Tirupati Tirumala Devasthanams (Financial assistance).

Baruah U.L. (1982). *This is All India Radio- a handbook of radio broadcasting in India.* New Delhi: Director General, Publications Division, Ministry of Information & Broadcasting, Govt. Of India.

List of Sanskrit Manuscripts in Private Libraries in South India, Vol I and Vol II. (1880,1885). Madras: Government Press.

Mani, V. (1975). *Puranic Encylopaedia.* Delhi: Motilal Banarasidas.

Maurice L. Ettinghausen M.R. (1906). *Harsa Vardhana, Empereur et poete de L*inde Septentrionale (606–648 A.D.).* Louvain: Doctoral Thesis , University of Paris.

Misra, Narayana. (2011). *Panninyavyakaranasutravritti Kasika of Pt Vamana and Jayaditya.* Varanasi: Chaukhamba Prakashan.

Murty, M.L. (n.d.). Renigunta. *https://www.academia.edu/23704278/,* https: / / www.academia.edu / 23704278 / MLK_Renigunta_Text_1_.

Iyengar R.N. (Bengaluru). *Parasaratantra.* 2013: Jain University Press, Jakkasandra Post, Ramanagara District.

Pandurangan, A. (1998). Nalayira Tivviya Pirapantham through inscriptions. *Journal of the Ananthacharya Indological Research Institute Vol 1,* 67–74.

Raghavacharya. (1961). *Sri Suktam (Hindi translation).* Acharyagranthamala.

Raghavaiah, T. (2004). *Alvar's Divya Vaibhavam.* Tirupati: T.T.D. Religious Publications Series No: 640.

Raghavan, S.P. (1983). *Vishnusaharanama Bhashya.* Madras (Chennai): Shri Visishtadvaita Pracharini Sabha.

Raghavan, V., Raja, K.K., Veezhinathan, N., Ramabai, E.R., Dash, S., & authors, A. (1949-2014). *New catalogus catalogorum: an alphabetical register of Sanskrit and allied works and authors.* Madras/Chennai: Madras University Sanskrit series, no. 18, 26, 28–35, 37–65, University of Madras.

Rajagopalachariar, T. (1909). *The Vaishnavite Reformers of India.* Madras: G.A. Natesan & Co,. Esplanade, Madras.

Ramanujam, V.V., Prof. (n.d.). Prathivadi Bhayankaram Anna Vaibhavam.

Ramanujam, B.V. (1973). *History of Vaishnavism in South India upto Ramanuja.* Annamalainagar: Annamalai University.

Ramanujan, V.V. (n.d.). *Life of Sri Ramanuja.*

Ramesan, N. (1981). *The Tirumala Temple.* Tirupati: Tirumala Tirupati Devasthanams.

Ramesh, M.S. (2000). *The Festivals and Rituals at Tirumala Temple.* Chennai: TR Publications Pvt Ltd.

Rao, S.K. (1993). *The Hill-Shrine of Vengadam.* Bangalore: Kalpatharu Research Academy.

Rasheed, C.B. (1907). *The Traveller's Companion containing a brief description of places of pilgrimage.* Calcutta: Railway Board, Govt. of India Press.

Sastry, S.S. (1998). *Report on the Inscriptions of the Devasthanam Collection with Illustrations.* Tirupati: TTD Epigraphical Series, Tirumala Tirupati Devasthanams.

Sastry, S.S. (1998). *Inscriptions of Saluva Narasimha's Time From 1445 AD to 1504 AD* . Tirupati: TTD Inscriptions Vol. 11, Tirumala Tirupati Devasthanams. *Inscriptions of Achyutadeva Raya's Time—From 1530 to 1542 AD.* Translated and Edited by Pandit V. Raghavacharya, TTD, Tirupati (1998).

Schrader, F.O. (1916). *Introduction to the Pancaratra and the Ahirbudhanya Samhita.* Madras: Adyar Library, Adyar.

Seymour, R., Schultze-Motel, P. Thermoregulating lotus flowers. *Nature* 383, 305 (1996). https://doi.org/10.1038/383305a0

Sherwani H.K, Joshi P.M. (ed), *The History of Medieval Deccan*, Govt. of Andhra Pradesh (1974).

Srinivasa Chari, P.N. (1946). *The Philosophy of Visistadvaita*, The Adyar Library, Adyar.

Srinivasa Chari, S.M. (2005). *Vaishnavism, its Philosophy, Theology and Religious Discipline.* Delhi: Motilal Banarsidass Publishers.

Srinivasa Rao, V.N. (1949). *Tirupati Sri Venkatesvara-Balaji.* Madras: Umadevan & Co.

Srinivasachari, S.M. (2005). *Vaisnavism- Its Philosophy,Theology and Religious Discipline.* Delhi: Motilal Banarasidass.

Srinivasan, C.K. (1944). *Maratha Rule in the Carnatic.* Annamalainagar: Annamalai University.

Srivari Brahmotsavam A celestial spectacle on Earth. (n.d.). Chennai: *The Hindu*.

Stein, B. (1960). The Economic Function of a Medieval South Indian Temple. *Journal of Asian Studies, Vol. 19, No 2*, 163–176 DOI: 10.2307/2943547 www.jstor.org/stable/2943547. Accessed 20 May 2020.

Subbarayalu, Y. (2016). A Note on Grammatical Knowledge in Early Tamilakam. *Indian Journal of the History of Science, 51.1*, 125–130.

Suryanarayana, K.V. (Vol. 45, No. 3,Feb. 5, 1976). The Eparchean Unconformity at Tirumalai—A Study. *Current Science*, pp. 86–88 see at https://www.currentscience.ac.in/php/show_ article.php?volume=045&issue=03&titleid= id_045_03_0086_0088_0&page=0086.

V. Rangachari (April 1917). The History of Sri Vaishnavaism (contd). *The Quarterly Journal of the Mythic Society, Vol. VII, No 3*, 197–209.

Varadachari V., *Buddhist Contribution to Sanskrit Literature*, Journal of the SVU ORI (1960), Vol. 3, p. 24.

Varadachari, V. (1982). *Agamas and South Indian Vaisnavism.* Chennai: Prof M Rangacharya Memorial Trust, Triplicane, Madras.

Vasantha, P. (2008). *Mahants of Hathiramji Mutt, 1843–1933.* Tirupati: PhD Thesis, Dept of History, SVU College of International Studies, Sri Venkateswara University.

Vedantham, R. (2008). *A Basic Study of Hinduism.* Chennai: R. Vedantham.

Viraraghavacharya, T.K.T. (2003). *History of Tirupati (The Tiruvengadam temples) in 3 volumes.* Tirupati: Tirumala Tirupati Devasthanams.

Vogel, J.P. (1908–09). *The Garuda Pillar of Besnagar.* Calcutta: Annual Report, Archaeological Society of India.

Wilks, C.M. (1817). *Historical Sketches Of The South of India in an attempt to trace the History of MYsoor: Vol II.* London: Longman. Hurst, Rees, Orme and Brown.

The Hindu Archives

Mirella Levi D'Ancona (1950). 'An Indian Statuette from Pompeii'. *Artibus Asiae,* Vol. 13, No. 3, pp. 166-180. https://www.jstor.org/stable/3248502

Orme, R. *The History of the Military Transaction of the British Nation in Indostan,* Vol. 1

Sastri, K.A. Nilakanta (1998) *A History of South India - From Prehistoric Times to the Fall of Vijayanagar.* Delhi: Oxford University Press.

Abbreviations

Sri Venkatachala Mahatmayam. Tirupati: Tirmala Tirupati Devasthanams. (1959–60): *VM.*

Iyengar, S.K. (1939). *A History of the Holy Shrine of Sri Venkateśa in Tirupati (Two volumes).* Madras: Printed at Ananda Press, *Sakkotai.*

Viraraghavacharya, T.K.T. (2003). *History of Tirupati (The*

Tiruvengadam temples) in 3 volumes. Tirupati: Tirumala Tirupati Devasthanams: *TKTV.*

Varadachari, V. (1982). *Agamas and South Indian Vaisnavism.* Chennai: Prof M Rangacharya Memorial Trust, Triplicane, Madras: *Varadachari, Agamas.*

Schrader, F.O. (1916). *Introduction to the Pancaratra and the Ahirbudhanya Samhita.* Madras: Adyar Library, Adyar: *Schrader.*

Ramachadra Rao, S.K. (1993). *The Hill-Shrine of Vengadam.* Bangalore: Kalpatharu Research Academy: *Ramachandra Rao, The Hill Shrine.*

Ramesan, N. (1981). *The Tirumala Temple.* Tirupati: Tirumala Tirupati Devasthanams: *Ramesan.*

Mani, V. (1975). *Puranic Encylopaedia.* Delhi: Motilal Banarasidas: *PE.*

Rajagopalachariar, T. (1909). *The Vaishnavite Reformers of India.* Madras: G.A. Natesan & Co,. Esplanade, Madras: *Rajagopalachariar, Vaishnavite Reformers.*

Yateendra Pravana Prabhavam edited by Ramanujam V.V.: *YPP.*

NOTES

Section One

1. See Raghavacharya K.V., Introduction *Sri Venkateśa Suprabhata Manajri Varivasya Vyakhya Sahitamau,* translated by Mahadeva Sarma p. 16.
2. Ibid, p. 17.
3. Ettinghausen M.R. (1906). *Harsa Vardhana, Empereur et poete de L*inde Septentrionale (606–648 A.D.).* Louvain: Doctoral Thesis , University of Paris. pp. 170–174. The author is grateful to Ms Nirada Harendra for the translation into English. Also please see Varadachari V., 'Buddhist contribution to Sanskrit Literature' Journal of the SVU ORI (1960), Vol. 3, p. 24.
4. Sri Ramachandra was a teenager when he volunteered to protect Vishwamitra's hermitage In an earlier chapter Dasharatha protested ऊनषोडशवर्षो मे रामो (my Rama is not yet sixteen) when asked by Vishwamitra, see Balakandam, chapter 20 verse 1.20.2.
5. Parasara Bhatta, *Vishnu Sahasranama Bhashya,* Visishtadvaita Pracharini Sabha p. 333.
6. Srinivasachari, *Vashnavism,* pp. 7–10.
7. Ibid. p. 11.
8. See Narayana Misra, *Paniniyavyakaransutravritti Kasika* 4.3.98 *vāsudevārjunābhyāṃ vun,* Chaukhamba (2011) p. 376.
9. See report by Vogel in *ASI annual report* 1908–09 pp. 126-129.
10. P. Bhatta, *Vishnusahasranamabhashya,* p. 295.

11. Ibid. p. 387.
12. See Raghavacharya, *Sri Suktam.*
13. See J.N. Banerjea, *Development of Hindu Iconography*, Univ. of Calucutta, 1941, p. 124.
14. See D'Ancona, M. (1950). An Indian Statuette from Pompeii. *Artibus Asiae, 13*(3), 166-180. doi:10.2307/3248502.
15. Swami Adidevananda Ramanuja Bhashya, pp. 464–467.
16. For more on the two versions of the story please see Sridhara Babu D., *Hayagriva The Horse-Headed Diety in Indian Culture*, SVUORI (1980) pp. 23–25.
17. Mani V., PE, pp. 365–366.
18. Jayaraj, Early *Hunter Gatherers* etc. pp 8–9.
19. Suryanarayana K.V., Eparchaen Unconformity, *Current Science*, Vol. 45, No. 3. Feb. 1976, pp. 86–88.
20. The length of a yojana is the subject of continuing research. The distance between Vijaywada (which is on the Krishna river) and Tirupati (on the Suvarnamukhi river) as the crow flies is around 346 kms.
21. *Venkatachala Mahatmayama,* M 1, p. 278 Padma Purana Kshetra khanda ch. 34 v. 4–14.
22. See for example Jacob Jayaraj, *Early Hunter Gatherers,* p. 55 onwards.
23. Murty, M.L.K., *Renigunta*. p. 474. https://www.academia.edu/23704278/MLK_Renigunta_Text_1_
24. This book uses the translation done by the late Sri Srirama Bharati – one of the greatest modern scholars of the Four Thousand.
25. See for example Srinivasachari, P.N, *The Philosophy of Visistadvaita* p. 504.
26. Means Holy end and start (अन्त + आदि) as the last word of a verse would be the first of the next.
27. Subbarayulu Y., 'A note on grammatical knowledge in early Tamilakam', *IJHS,* 51.1(2016) p. 128. Also S.K. Iyengar *The History etc.* Vol. 1, pp. 14–18.
28. See Jagadeesan, N: *Collected papers on Tamil Vaishnavism,* Vaishnavism in the Sangam age p. 3. It also meant the

sea, a water-bearing cloud, the blue lily etc and therefore provided poets a lot of scope for building imagery around descriptions of the God.

29. Ibid. p. 26.
30. Ibid. p. 29.
31. See S.K. Iyengar, (Founder of Tirupati) in *The History etc*, Vol. 1, Ch. 2, pp. 40–51.
32. TKTV Vol. 1, p. 92. Also Ramesan 'Tirumala in Silappadhikaram', p. 53.
33. See for example *Srirama Bharati* Mudal Tiruvandadi of Poygai Alvar, pp. 626–636.
34. *Srirama Bharati* Irandu Tiruvandadi of Bootatt Alvar, pp. 637–652.
35. *Srirama Bharati* Munram Tiruvadadi of Pey Alva, pp. 652–667.
36. Ibid, pp. 667–682 and then pp. 209–213.
37. *Sri Vishnu Puranam* 3.1.32, p. 186. A huge corpus of work exists for the concept of time in India through the ages. The system is described in simple Sanskrit in the Vishnu Purana (First section, third chapter).
38. Vettam Mani, *Puranic Encyclopaedia (PE).*
39. *PE* pp. 74–75.
40. *PE* pp. 117–118.
41. *PE* pp. 285–286.
42. *PE* pp. 339–341.
43. *PE* pp. 396–398.
44. *PE* pp. 834–836.
45. *PE* pp. 872–977.
46. Dikshit S.B., *History of Indian Astronomy* vol. 1, pp. 55–56.
47. *Brihat Samhita* 13.1–2, p. 155.
48. Sakkotai p. 219 onwards.
49. See TKTV Vol. 1, pp. 72–80 for details about the period.
50. TKTV Vol. 1, pp. 96–102. Also Ramesan pp. 21–22.
51. Ramachandra Rao S.K., *The Hill Shrine*, p. 33.
52. Ramanujan, B.V., *History of Vaishnavism in South India upto Ramanuja* p. 247 and p. 267.

53. Ibid. pp. 254–264. Others state that Yamunacharya was born in 916 CE. For example see Raghavachariar, *Vaishnavite Reformers*, p. 10.
54. V. Varadachari, *Agamas and South Indian Vaishnavism* (1982), pp. 9–11.
55. Varadachari, *Agamas etc.* pp. 80–85.
56. Otto Schrader F., *Introduction to Pancaratra etc.* p. 11. Schrader was an extraordinary man. He was the German Director of the Adyar Library, Madras and was interned as an enemy alien during WWI, but not before he had finished his study.
57. Varadachari V., *Agamas etc.* p. 117.
58. See Pandurangan *in Journal of AIRI* I–1998, pp. 67–74.
59. See Govindacharya, *Life of Ramanujacharya*, pp. 6–8 for more on Nathamuni's musical prowess.
60. See chapter on Nathamuni in Rajagopalachariar, *Vaishnavite Repormers,* pp. 1–11.
61. Many of the great teachers started very young—for example both Sankaracharya and Madhvacharya had mastered all there was to learn by their teens.
62. Govindacharya A., *Life of Ramanuja* p. 20.
63. Rajagopalachariar, *Vaishnavite Reformers* p. 35.
64. Ibid. p. 48.
65. Ibid. p. 49.
66. Ibid. p. 47.
67. The TTD has helpfully labelled various trees for those interested.
68. See Rajagopalachari, *Vaishnava reformers* etc. p. 51.
69. See Govindacharya A., *Ramanuja* pp. 34–36.
70. See Rajagopalachari, *Vaishnava reformers* etc. p. 76 and V.V. Ramanujan, *Life of Sri Ramanuja.*
71. The standard biography of Ramanujacharya in English is by A. Govindacharya and is now more than a century old. V.V. Ramanujan has contributed a more recent work.

Section Two

72. Dave, K.N, , *Birds in Indian Literature,* MLBD 2005 pp. 141–145.
73. The date is stated with great confidence as 24 Feb 1130 by TKTV, Vol. 1, p. 250 and by V.V. Ramanujam, *Life of Sri Ramanuja.*
74. Jagannatha, Sarojini, *Impact of Ramanujacharya* etc. pp. 130–147.
75. For a very detailed description of temple administration in pre-Vijaynagar times see Ramesan pp. 312–351.
76. Ramesan pp. 321–327.
77. See Ibn Batuta, *Rehla,* pp. 227–229., trans. M. Hasan, Oriental Institute Baroda,1976.
78. See for example Sakkotai, Vol. 1, p. 392 or pp. 404–405.
79. Sakkotai in Vol. 1, pp. 412–416.
80. TKTV, Vol. 1, p. 212.
81. Sarangadeva, *Sangeeta Ratnakara,* part 2, Anandashram Press (1942) verse 9–10, p. 480.
82. The sixty-year cycle of years in the Indian calendar is named after them.
83. For many stories about Narada, see Vettam Mani, *PE,* pp. 526–530.
84. Rajagolachariar, *Vaishnavite Reformers,* p. 102.
85. See Rajagopalacharia. C.,*Vaishnavite Reformers,* pp. 119–120. Also see *Prapannaamritam* p. 466 to p. 471.
86. Kampanna is the hero of the historical poem *Madhuravijayam* composed by his wife Gangadevi.
87. For the life of Manavala Mahamuni please see Rajagopalachari, *Vaishnavite Reformers,* pp. 132–135.
88. Seymour, R., Schultze-Motel, P. Thermoregulating lotus flowers. *Nature* 383, 305 (1996). https://doi.org/10.1038/383305a0.
89. Ediriweera E., Premarathna N. Medicinal and cosmetic uses of Bee's Honey—A review. *AYU* [serial online] 2012

[cited 2019 Apr 10]; 33:178–82. Available from: http://www.ayujournal.org/text.asp?2012/33/2/178/105233.

90. For a definitive work on bees in Sanskrit Lit., see Karttunen, K. (2015). Bhramarotpītādharaḥ: Bees in Classical India. *Studia Orientalia Electronica, 107*, 89–134. Retrieved from https://journal.fi/store/article/view/52400.
91. See Ibid p. 103. The section on bees visiting flowers at night in this paper concludes by mentioning that rather than bees other nocturnal insects visited flowers at night.
92. TKTV, Vol. 2, p. 397.
93. See TKTV, Vol. 2, 389–405 for extensive details about Narasimha's contribution to the Tirumala Temple.
94. I am grateful to his son Professor V. Anandamurthy for his memories as well as all the other details of the Tallapaka poets. He was kind enough to host me for a two-session lecture on the Tallapaka poets and their association with the Venkateśa Suprabhātam at his house in RR Nagar, Bangalore.
95. It is still part of colloquial usage. For example a group of ladies maybe be referred to as *madam-log* in Hindi.
96. I am grateful for P.B. Sampath for taking the time to accompany me to Sitarambagh and for making the introductions to the Swamyji.
97. Also known as Swamy Kumara Varadacharya in many accounts.
98. For the verse in Sanskrit see P.B.A. Varadachariar *Anna Vaibhavam* issued for Sri Pradivaadhi Bayankaram Anna Swami's 651st Birth Anniversary.
99. This work is considered by many to be among Anna's best.
100. As per V.V. Ramanujam's hagiography on Anna, p. 15.
101. See first few verses of the *Vādibhīkaraguruparamparāślokāḥ* and also see Sri Pradivaadhi Bayankaram Anna Swami's 651st Birth Anniversary. Vaibhavam by P.B.A.V. Swamy, p. 4.

102. An incomplete version in the Grantha script is in the author's possession.
103. The author is grateful to P.B. Phaninder and P.B. Sampath in Hyderabad for all their help.
104. *Vijayraghavacharya* trans. by M. Sarma p. 40. The Professor has cited from the Markandeya Purana.
105. YPP is thought to have been composed in the 16th century and is edited by the indefatigable Dr V.V. Ramanujam. I am also grateful to my cousin Mrs Kalyani Sridhar for the translation.
106. Dates could not be ascertained by this author. A more scholarly foray could well result in greater certainity.
107. Rangachari,V. *The History of Vaishnavism,* Mythic Society, Bangalore (1917) p. 205.
108. See for example Ibid. pp. 205–207.
109. TKTV Vol. 1, pp. 211–212.
110. YPP, pp. 155–156.
111. Basavaraju, Sridhar V. *The Priests of Tirumala,* pp. 36–41.
112. Incriptions of Saluva Narasimha's time, TTD Publications Vol. 2, Inscription no. 4 (no. 3–TT) pp. 6–8. Also Sastry S.S., Report on Inscriptions of the Devasthanam Collections with illustrationsTirupati, TTD (1998), p. 12.
113. Introductory note no. 59, *Kainkarayaratnavalli* pp. 38–39.
114. Sakkotai, Vol. 2, pp. 108–109.
115. Sakkotai, Vol. 2, p. 118. For the shortest account see Ramesan pp. 364–368. On the other hand, Sakkotai and TKTV have written a few chapters each.
116. TKTV, Vol. 2, p. 444.
117. Ibid. p. 428.
118. For the detailed chronology of the Tallapaka poets see Anandamurthy V, *'Andhra Sahtiyamupai Vishnu mata Prabhavamu' Vol. 2, Tallapka Kavulu.* Thesis in Tuelugu, Reprinted in 2017, Subhodaya Foundation, Kakinada, pp. 56–64.
119. Sastri S.S. *TTD Epigraphical report.* pp. 283–284.

120. Interview with Prof. V. Anandamurthy. A printed version of the Venkateśa Prabhatastavamu can be seen in the book V. Prabhakara Sastri (edited by), *Sri Venkatesvara Vachanamulu with Sri Venkatesvara Prabhatastavamu* by Tallapaka Peddatirumalacharyulu, Sri Venkatesvara Oriental Series, No. 10, 1946, Tirumala Tirupati Devasthanams.
121. See verses 39 to 65 in the first Ch. Bhavishyottara Purana in *Venkatachala Mahatmayam,* Vol. 2, pp. 264–266.
122. See verses 67 to 81 in ibid, pp. 267–268.
123. See verses 12 to 51 in Brahma Purana chapter 1 and verses 1 to 13 in chapter 2 in *Venkatachala Mahatmayam,* Vol. 2, pp. 2–8.
124. See verses 82 to 127 in the first Ch Bhavishyottara Purana in *Venkatachala Mahatmayam,* Vol. 2, pp. 268–272.
125. See verses 128 to 220 in ibid. pp. 272–280.
126. See TKTV, Vol. 2, pp. 468–470.
127. Sastri S.S., *Tirupati Devasthanam Epigraphical Report,* p. 193, citing inscription 497-TT.
128. Sastri S.S., *TTD Epigraphical Report,* pp. 280–290.
129. See chapter on Achyuta Deva Raya's reign TKTV, Vol. 2, pp. 467–512.
130. See Stein, Burton. 'The Economic Function of a Medieval South Indian Temple', *The Journal of Asian Studies,* Vol. 19, No. 2, 1960 footnote in p. 169.
131. TKTV, Vol. 2, pp. 502–503. There were consistent and clear practices ruling every aspect of the 'laws of contracts' among the Indian mercantile communities from very early in Indian history. A preferred divinity used to be the witness to the contract and this placed a very high burden of non-compliance among the contracting parties as the penalties of breach followed into after-life.
132. Also see Inscription no 112 (148–GT) in *Inscriptions of Achyutadeva Raya's Time,* pp. 208–210.

Section Three

133. Nilakanta Sastri, p. 289.
134. Nilakanta Sastri, p. 295.
135. Nilakanta Sastri, p. 312.
136. TKTV, pp. 579–580.
137. *PE*, pp. 10–15.
138. *PE*, pp. 318–328.
139. *PE*, p. 367–370.
140. *PE*, pp. 434–437.
141. *PE*, pp. 832–833.
142. *PE*, pp. 840–841.
143. Sakkotai, Vol. 2, p. 321.
144. *Illustrated History of the South Indian Railway*, Higginbotham & Co, p. 327.
145. TKTV, Vol. 2, pp. 588–591.
146. TKTV, p. 581.
147. TKTV, Vol. 2, p. 593.
148. For a definitive account of this period see the section on Vijayanagara in *The History of Medieval Deccan* edited by Sherwani and Joshi, p. 136.
149. Ramesh M.S., pp. 62–64.
150. Varaha Purana chapter 51, Verse 5, p. 79 in the *Venkatachala Mahatmayam* part 1 (TTD) for the list of mounts and Ch. 50 and 51 pp. 72–79 for other details of the festival. For the best exposition of this festival in Tirumala see M.S. Ramesh *Festivals and Rituals of Tirumala* pp. 66–140.
151. Ramesh M.S., p. 74 and p. 78.
152. *PE*, pp. 281–285.
153. Ramesh M.S., p. 78.
154. *Srivari Brahmotsavam*, p. 7.
155. Ramesh M.S., p. 78.
156. *PE*, p. 800.
157. Ramesh M.S., p. 79.
158. *The Hindu Srivari Brahmotsavam*, p. 8.

159. Ramesh M.S., pp. 78–79.
160. Srirama Bharati, pp. 212–213.
161. See section on the Qutub Shahis of Golconda–Hyderabad in *History of Medieval Deccan* edited by Sherwani and Joshi, pp. 411–491.
162. *Storia do Mogor,* Vol. 3, p. 143 trans. W. Irvine, 1907.
163. TKTV, Vol. II, p. 611.
164. TKTV, Vol. 3, p. 11.
165. TKTV, Vol. II, pp. 617–624. Prasad P.V.R.K. in *When I Saw Tirupati Balaji,* p. 134 states that in earlier times, the officiating priests used to live in Tirupati and would trek up every day regardless of how many devotees visited the Temple.
166. For a deep dive into such topics please see Iyengar, R.N., *Parasaratantra.*
167. For Surya see *PE,* pp. 770–772 and for Chandra *PE,* pp. 171–172.
168. *PE,* pp. 760–761.
169. Apte V.S., *The Practical Sanskrit-English Dictionary*, p. 922.
170. *PE,* p. 477.
171. Iyengar R.N., *Parasaratantra,* p. 104.
172. *PE,* pp. 162–164.
173. *PE,* p. 626.
174. Iyengar R.N., *Parasaratantra,* pp. 86–100.
175. *Brihat Samhita,* p. 127 onwards.
176. Iyengar R.N., *Parasaratantra,* pp. 126–149.
177. See Preface to note on *New Catalogus Catalogum* by Sastri, Sastri, Raja. Woolner's personal collection of Sanskrit manuscripts is currently housed in the Punjab University, Lahore.
178. See *New Catalogus Catalogorum* XXXI, p. 120.
179. Ibid. p. 117.
180. See for example listings under *Venkateshastuti* in NCC Vol. XXXI, p. 122.
181. See manuscript of the *Venkateśa Suprabhātam,* Folio 66435, Adyar Library and Research Centre.

182. Govindacharya A., *The Holy Lives of the Azhvaars,* pp. 1–18.
183. See description of Manuscript No. R 6396 *Trennial catalogue of the GOML,* Volume X, Sanskrit–A, Govt Press, Madras, 1950, p. 8097.
184. Ramanujam, V.V., *Anna Vaibhavam,* p. 13.
185. Ramachandra Rao, S.K., *The Hill Shrine of Vengadam,* Introduction.
186. Ibid. p. 62.
187. Ibid. p. 67.
188. Ibid. p. 69.
189. Ibid. p. 72.
190. Ibid. pp. 91–92.
191. Ibid. pp. 121–122.
192. Ibid. pp. 165–166.
193. See V.V. Subramanya Kumar pp. 40–41. By this time many from other parts of India were a factor in peninsular affairs. While the Maratha rules of Tanjore and Rajput commanders of the Senji fort are best known there were many others. For example, the story of the Bukkanji family of bankers who apparently dealt with everyone who was anyone—the French, the English, the Nawab of Carnatic, and the Tirumala Temple—would be a fascinating one to trace.
194. Or Nazeabulla Cawn as he is called by Robert Orme throughout Vol. 1, Book 4, pp. 321–323 of *The Military etc.*
195. TKTV, Vol. 2, pp. 633–635.
196. To get a feel of the chaos during the times see TKTV, pp. 632–642.
197. Hyder Ali had refused to meddle in Tirumala and was therefore derided by the English for his 'more than half-Hindoo propensities [that] had induced him to grant unqualified indemnity to the sacred temple of Tripety' by Wilks in *Historical Sketches of South of India,* Vol. 2, p. 349.
198. Srinivasa Rao, V.N., *Tirupati Sri Venkateswara,* p. 167.

199. In 1803. Ibid. p. 190.
200. Ramesan pp. 504–506.
201. See Ramesan p. 510.
202. For example see Rangaswamy A., 'Traditional Music-Development in Tirupati', *The Hindu* 13 March 1961, p. 12.
203. Chapter on *Dasavataras.* 22 avataras in *the Bhagavatam.* Book 1 Chapter 3 verse 10 onwards (सूत उवाच ... जगृहे पौरूषं रूपम ...).
204. Srinivasachari, P.N., *The Philosophy of Visistadvaita* p. 154.
205. Varadachari, p. 318.
206. Schrader, p. 52.
207. Srinivasa Chari S.M., *Vaishnavism* pp. 187–190.
208. Ibid., pp. 191–198.
209. Vasantha P., *The Mahants of Hathiramji Mutt,* pp. 13–15.
210. Vasantha P., *The Mahants of Hathiramji Mutt,* p. 19.
211. Vasantha P., *The Mahants of the Hathiramji Mutt,* 1843–1933, pp. 16–17.
212. Ramesan, p. 551.
213. See Special Lecture in Telugu by A.V. Srinivasacharyulu as a part of the proceedings of 26 October 1998 recorded in Appendix 3 of *the Tirumala Music Inscriptions* ed., V. Anandamurthy, p. 10. Translated by Sri Mahadeva Sarma.
214. *NCC,* Vol. XXXI, p. 120.
215. *The Traveller's Companion,* Railway Board (1907) p. 250.
216. Vasantha P., *The Mahants etc.,* p. 281.

Section Four

217. E.g., Narsingha Mehta.
218. Those interested in an authoritative and lucid general explanation of the underlying philosophy of this prayer may see *The Philosophy of Visistadvaita* by P.N. Srinivasachari, Adyar (1943).
219. Srinivasa Chari S.M., *Vaishnavism,* pp. 212–217.
220. Baruah U.L.,*This is All India Radio,* pp. 10–18.

221. Apparently, this box set is a collector's item if one were to go by mentions in cyberspace.
222. Thanks are owed to Mr Atmanathan 'Atma Sir'—one of the most helpful among the helpful strangers—for helping me connect to them.
223. Thirumalai, 'The Man who Woke God', *The Times of India*, 10 June 1976.
224. Varadachari, *Agamas* pp. 347–348.
225. Ramachandra Rao S.K., *The Hill Shrine*, pp. 219–222.
226. Ramachandra Rao S.K., *The Hill Shrine*, p. 223.
227. Ibid., p. 243 and p. 233.
228. Ibid., p. 242.
229. Ibid., pp. 228–230.
230. Since film music and cricket commentaries were not seen to be furthering such lofty goals, they were banished to Radio Ceylon.
231. George T.J.S., *MS: A Definitive Biography*, Aleph (2016), p. 178.
232. *The Hindu*, 21 December 1958.
233. This para is a transcription of an interview with Mr V. Shrinivasan, Mrs Subbulakshmi's grandson.
234. *Bhagavata Purana*, 1.3.5–25.
235. For descriptions of many avataras, see Schrader, *Introduction to Pancharatra* pp. 42–48 and for just a listing Srinivasa Chari S M, *Vaishnavism* p. 219.
236. Some of the above paragraphs as well as some of the other anecdotes relating to MS Amma and the Venkateśa Suprabhātam were recounted by Mr V Shrinivasan who met me at an hour's notice and then proceeded to spend two hours talking about what he remembered.
237. 'Elevating role of Music—AIR Sammelan in Delhi', *The Hindu*, 3 Nov 1963, p. 7.
238. 'Slokas pictured in Paintings', *The Hindu*, 5 Sep 1975.
239. Ramesh M.S., *Festivals and Rituals of Tirumala.*
240. For the entire sequence see section on Suprabhataseva in Festivals etc. M.S. Ramesh, pp. 202–206.

241. See Ramesh M.S., p. 204.
242. *The Hindu*,14 Sep 1990, p. 3. Some parts of this section are as per interview with Mr V. Shrinivasan.
243. The translation of the TE done by the late Sri Srirama Bharati has been used for the purpose of comparison.
244. 'The Song of Dawn', A.J. Phillip, *The Tribune*, 13 December 2004. https://www.tribuneindia.com/2004/20041213/edit.htm#5. The author is grateful to Mr V. Shrinivasan for pointing out this article.
245. Ramnarayan, Gowri, 'Recording a Legend', *The Hindu* 17 Sep 2010.
246. Those interested can visit https://ttdsevaonline.com/#/login for more details.
247. For details see Prasad P.V.R.K., 'Anjaneya rises on the Anjanadri', *When I saw Tirupati Balaji*, pp. 161–169.
248. https://economictimes.indiatimes.com/news/politics-and-nation/coronavirus-tirupati-balaji-temple-to-be-shut-for-devotees/articleshow/74717538.cms?from=mdr

ACKNOWLEDGEMENTS

Between the first edition of this book and this one, I lost many of my mentors and guides – Sri Mahadeva Sarma, Prof. U. Ve M.A. Lakshmithathacharya Swamy of Melkote and Prof. Raghavacharya who walked this path in Telugu much before I did. This edition is a tribute to their memory.

This book could not have been written without the blessing of my parents and the grace of their best friend and guide in all matters which is Lord Venkateswara himself.

The journey would have been impossible without the guidance of my teachers particularly Smt. Prabha Anant and Sri Mahadeva Sarma.

In some ways this book is a tribute to the members and employees of TTD (many of whom helped me) and to all those who have stood and served the devotees without expectation in the past.

The Sitarambagh Swamyji, Sriman P.B. Annangaracharyulu (Hyderabad), Sri P.B. Phanindar and Sri P.B. Sampath were most helpful among the descendants of P.B. Anna, and I am grateful to them for their help and friendship. Prof. Veturi Anandamurthy was kind enough to talk me though the history of the Tallapaka poets. Sri V. Shrinivasan and members of the late P.V. Anantasayanam's family, spent a lot of time talking through the anecdotes and experiences of MS Amma and P.V. Anantasayanam Iyengar respectively. Smt. Gowri Ramnarayan, Atmanathan Sir, 'HMV Raghu' Sir, Vikram Mehra, T. Anand and the team at Saregama Chennai were helpful with time, anecdotes and connections.

Prof. N.C.B. Nath and Sunder Chakravarthy were encouraging with comments and suggestions as were N.P. Sridhar, Nirada Harenda and my aunt, Dr Vasantha.

Prof. R.N. Iyengar shared the research corpus on temples of south India which had been collected by his sister, the late

Prof. R. Vasantha. Prof. K.V. Raman was kind enough to tell me his thoughts on temples and Vaishnavism generally, over a cup of a coffee at his residence in Chennai. Dr U.Ve.P. Ramanujan swamy and Prof. U.Ve.V.S. Vijayaraghavan swamy helped me with the grantha transliteration of the prayer.

Prof. U.Ve.M.A. Lakshmitathacharya, Dr Devangana Desai, Dr Naresh Keerthi, Dr Shesha Shastri, Ms Gayatri Ramachandran, Sri A.P.V.N. Sarma Garu and Dr Mukteswara Rao Garu for their help / comments / suggestions at various stages.

The teams at the various archives were helpful, particularly the team at GOML Archives in Chennai, the team at SVU ORI in Tirupati, the team at Kuppuswami Shastri research Institute in Chennai, the entire ALRC team at the Theosophical Society in Chennai, Sri B. Guruprasad at the B.M. Sri Pratishthana in Bangalore, and the librarian and team at the Hindu archives in Chennai. Smt. Srirama Bharati and her niece Radha helped out with a copy of Sri Srirama Bharati's standard work on the Naalayiram.

Many friends like Y. Sivagovardhan Reddy, Venu Madhav Vadlamani, the late Prof. C.S. Sheshadri, Prof. Gautam Bharali played a part in various ways. Manisha Sobhrajani, Amish Mulmi and Kanishka Gupta were instrumental in the first few steps.

My editor Karthik Venkatesh was a steadfast guide and I am deeply grateful to him for hand holding my first foray in writing. This book would not have seen the light of day without his steady support and persistence, his ability to keep me focussed and his infinite patience. The team at Westland Books saw through the last hard yards, despite the travails of Covid.

I am grateful to HarperCollins India for giving this book a second home. Rahul Soni, Amrita Mukerji, Mukul Chand and Rajatveer Singh were very supportive and burned the midnight oil (literally, too, as it was during Diwali time) to meet deadlines.

My cousin Kalyani was a big help—reading drafts, translating sources and ready to get on the phone on odd hours to talk.

Nothing would have been possible without the constant support of my wife and my son. They know what they did.

Finally, thanks are due to the many countless people who knowingly or unknowingly helped in this journey, starting with that nameless Tamil truck driver whom I ran across in Lunkaranasar on a bitterly cold winter morning in 1994.

ABOUT THE AUTHOR

Venkatesh Parthasarathy lives in Bangalore. He is interested in the history of peninsular India and is learning Sanskrit. This is his first book.

30 Years *of*

HarperCollins *Publishers* India

At HarperCollins, we believe in telling the best stories and finding the widest possible readership for our books in every format possible. We started publishing 30 years ago; a great deal has changed since then, but what has remained constant is the passion with which our authors write their books, the love with which readers receive them, and the sheer joy and excitement that we as publishers feel in being a part of the publishing process.

Over the years, we've had the pleasure of publishing some of the finest writing from the subcontinent and around the world, and some of the biggest bestsellers in India's publishing history. Our books and authors have won a phenomenal range of awards, and we ourselves have been named Publisher of the Year the greatest number of times. But nothing has meant more to us than the fact that millions of people have read the books we published, and somewhere, a book of ours might have made a difference.

As we step into our fourth decade, we go back to that one word – a word which has been a driving force for us all these years.

Read.

Harper Collins

4th

HARPER PERENNIAL

HARPER BUSINESS

HARPER BLACK

हार्पर हिन्दी

HarperCollins *Children's Books*

HARPER DESIGN

HARPER VANTAGE

Harper Sport